Hugo's Simplified System

Turkish
Phrase Book

Hugo's Language Books Limited

Compiled by
Lexus Ltd
with
Ahmet T Türkistanlı
and
Felicity J Ünlü

*Facts and figures given in this book were
correct when printed. If you discover any
changes, please write to us.*

5th impression 1995

Set in 9/9 Plantin Light by
Typesetters Ltd and
printed and bound in Great Britain
by Page Bros, Norwich

CONTENTS

CONTENTS

PREFACE

This Turkish Phrase Book has the same excellent pedigree as others in the Hugo series, having been compiled by experts to meet the general needs of tourists and business travellers. Arranged under the usual headings of 'Hotels', 'Motoring' and so forth, the ample selection of useful words and phrases is supported by a 2000-line mini-dictionary. By cross-reference to this, scores of additional phrases may be formed. There is also an extensive menu guide listing approximately 550 dishes or methods of cooking and presentation.

The pronunciation of words and phrases in the main text is imitated in English sound syllables, and highlighted sections illustrate some of the replies you may be given and the signs or instructions you may see or hear.

PRONUNCIATION

When reading the imitated pronunciation, stress that part which is underlined. Pronounce each syllable as if it formed part of an English word, and you will be understood sufficiently well. Remember the points below, and your pronunciation will be even closer to the correct Turkish. Use our audio cassette of selected extracts from this book, and you should be word-perfect!

ay   represents the Turkish 'ey' sound and is pronounced as in 'day'.

eh   is pronounced like the 'e' in 'led'.

'eye'   represents the Turkish 'ay' sound and is pronounced like the English word 'eye'.

ew   represents the Turkish 'ü' sound. This is like the French 'u' or the German 'ü'; pronounce it like the sound in 'few' or 'pew'.

s   is always pronounced as in 'pass', *never* as in 'easy'.

uh   represents the Turkish 'ı' sound and is pronounced like the 'i' in 'sir' or the 'er' sound in 'mother'.

ur   represents the Turkish 'ö' sound and corresponds to the German 'ö' which is like the 'ur' sound in 'further'.

SUMMARY OF SPECIAL TURKISH CHARACTERS

c   (without the cedilla underneath) like 'j' in 'jolly'.

ç   (with cedilla) 'ch' as in 'church'.

ğ   (with breve) is not a 'g' sound at all; it lengthens the preceding vowel.

ı   (looks like an undotted 'i') sounds *uh* – see above.

İ   is a dotted capital 'i'.

ö   (with diaeresis above) sounds *ur* – see above.

ş   (with cedilla) 'sh' as in 'ship'.

ü   (with diaeresis) as in 'few' – see above.

6

USEFUL EVERYDAY PHRASES

Yes/No
Evet/Hayır
evet/h-'eye'-uhr

Thank you
Teşekkür ederim
teshek-kewr edereem

No thank you
Hayır, teşekkür ederim
h-'eye'-uhr, teshek-kewr edereem

Please
Lütfen
lewtfen

I don't understand
Anlamıyorum
anlamuhyoroom

Do you speak English/French/German?
İngilizce/Fransızca/Almanca biliyor musunuz?
eengheeleez-jeh/franssuhz-ja/alman-ja beeleeyor moo-soonooz?

I can't speak Turkish
Türkçe bilmiyorum
tewrk-cheh beelmeeyoroom

Please speak more slowly
Lütfen daha yavaş konuşur musunuz?
lewtfen daha yavash konooshoor moo-soonooz?

USEFUL EVERYDAY PHRASES

Please write it down for me
Lütfen yazar mısınız?
lewtfen yazar muh-suh-nuhz?

Good morning
Günaydın
ghewn-'eye'-duhn

Good afternoon
İyi günler
eeyee ghewn-ler

Good evening
İyi akşamlar
eeyee akshamlar

Good night
İyi geceler
eeyee gheh-jeler

Hello
Merhaba
merhaba

Goodbye
Hoşça kalın
hosh-cha kaluhn

How are you?
Nasılsınız?
nassuhl-suhnuhz?

Excuse me please
Affedersiniz
af-federsseeneez

Sorry!
Özür dilerim!
urzewr deelereem!

I'm really sorry
Çok affedersiniz
chok af-federsseeneez

Can you help me?
Bana yardım edebilir misiniz?
bana yarduhm edebeeleer mee-seeneez?

Can you tell me ...?
... söyleyebilir misiniz?
... surleh-yebeeleer mee-seeneez?

Can I have ...?
... rica ediyorum
... reeja edeeyoroom

I would like ...
... istiyorum
... eesteeyoroom

Is there a ... here?
Burada ... var mı?
boorada ... var muh?

Where can I get ...?
... nerede bulabilirim?
... neh-reh-deh boolabeeleereem?

How much is it?
Bunun fiyatı ne kadar?
boonoon fee-yatuh neh kadar?

USEFUL EVERYDAY PHRASES

What time is it?
Saat kaç?
Sa-at kach?

I must go now
Şimdi gitmem lazım
sheemdee gheetmem la-zuhm

Cheers!
Şerefe!
sherefeh!

Do you take credit cards?
Kredi kartı kabul ediyor musunuz?
kredee kartuh kabool edeeyor moo-soonooz?

Can I pay by cheque?
Çekle ödeyebilir miyim?
chekleh urdeh-yebeeleer mee-yeem?

Where are the toilets?
Tuvaletler nerede?
toovaletler neh-reh-deh?

Go away!
Çekil!
chekeel!

It's hot/cold today
Bugün hava sıcak/soğuk
booghewn hava suhjak/so-ook

Excellent!
Çok güzel!
chok ghewzel!

THINGS YOU'LL SEE OR HEAR

açık	open
afiyet olsun!	enjoy your meal
allahaısmarladık	goodbye *(said by person leaving)*
arkada	at the back
aşağıda	at the bottom, downstairs
ayrılmış	reserved
basamağa dikkat	mind the step
bayanlar	ladies
baylar	gentlemen
bedava	free
bozuk	out of order
buyurun	please *(meaning 'come in', 'sit down', 'go ahead' etc)*
cadde	street
çalınız	ring
çekiniz	pull
çıkış	way out
çocuklar	children
...-den	from ...
dikkat	attention
dikkat ediniz	take care
döviz	foreign currency
dur	stop
efendim	sir/madam
efendim?	I beg your pardon?
erkekler	men
fiat, fiyat	price
giriniz	enter
giriş	way-in, entry
güle güle	goodbye *(said by person remaining behind)*
gümrük	customs
hızlı	fast

⟶

hoş geldiniz!	welcome! (*you reply:* ***hos bulduk*** *meaning 'a welcome found'*)
inşallah!	God willing!
itiniz	push
kadar	until
kadınlar	women
kalkış	departure
kapalı	closed
kasa	till, cash desk
kasaba	town
kiralamak	to rent/hire
kiralık	for rent
kontrol	check, inspection
lütfen	please
maşallah!	wonderful!
memnun oldum!	pleased to meet you
mesai saatleri	opening hours
meşgul	engaged
ödeyiniz	pay
önde	at the front
sağ	right
satılık	for sale
serbest	free
sigara içilmez	no smoking
sokak	street
sol	left
tarife	charges, price list, timetable
tehlike	danger
varış	arrival
vurunuz	knock
... yasaktır	... not allowed
yavaş	slow
yayalar	pedestrians
yetişkinler	adults
yok	there is none
yukarıda	at the top, above, upstairs

DAYS, MONTHS, SEASONS

Sunday	pazar	*pazar*
Monday	pazartesi	*pazartessee*
Tuesday	salı	*saluh*
Wednesday	çarşamba	*charshamba*
Thursday	perşembe	*pershembeh*
Friday	cuma	*jooma*
Saturday	cumartesi	*joomartessee*

January	ocak	*o-jak*
February	şubat	*shubat*
March	mart	*mart*
April	nisan	*neessan*
May	mayıs	*m-'eye'-uhss*
June	haziran	*hazeeran*
July	temmuz	*tem-mooz*
August	ağustos	*a-oostoss*
September	eylül	*ay-lewl*
October	ekim	*ekeem*
November	kasım	*kassuhm*
December	aralık	*araluhk*

Spring	ilkbahar	*eelk-bahar*
Summer	yaz	*yaz*
Autumn	sonbahar	*sonbahar*
Winter	kış	*kuhsh*

Christmas	Noel	*no-el*
Christmas Eve	Noel Gecesi	*no-el ghejessee*
Easter	Paskalya	*passkalya*
New Year	Yılbaşı	*yuhl-bashuh*
New Year's Eve	Yılbaşı Gecesi	*yuhl-bashuh ghejessee*

NUMBERS

0	sıfır *suhfuhr*	**5**	beş *besh*
1	bir *beer*	**6**	altı *altuh*
2	iki *eekee*	**7**	yedi *yedee*
3	üç *ewch*	**8**	sekiz *sekeez*
4	dört *durt*	**9**	dokuz *dokooz*

10	on *on*
11	on bir *on beer*
12	on iki *on eekee*
13	on üç *on ewch*
14	on dört *on durt*
15	on beş *on besh*
16	on altı *on altuh*
17	on yedi *on yedee*
18	on sekiz *on sekeez*
19	on dokuz *on dokooz*
20	yirmi *yeermee*
21	yirmi bir *yeermee beer*
22	yirmi iki *yeermee eekee*
30	otuz *otooz*
31	otuz bir *otooz beer*
32	otuz iki *otooz eekee*
40	kırk *kuhrk*
50	elli *el-lee*
60	altmış *altmuhsh*
70	yetmiş *yetmeesh*
80	seksen *sekssen*
90	doksan *dokssan*
100	yüz *yewz*
110	yüz on *yewz on*
200	iki yüz *eekee yewz*
1000	bin *been*
1,000,000	bir milyon *beer meel-yon*

14

TIME

today	bugün	boogh*ewn*
yesterday	dün	d*ewn*
tomorrow	yarın	yar*uhn*
the day before	evvelki gün	ev-v*elkee* gh*ewn*
the day after	öbür gün	urb*ewr* gh*ewn*
this week	bu hafta	boo haft*a*
last week	geçen hafta	gh*echen* haft*a*
next week	gelecek hafta	ghel*ejek* haft*a*
this morning	bu sabah	boo sab*ah*
this afternoon	bugün öğleden sonra	boogh*ewn* url*eden* s*o*nra
this evening	bu akşam	boo aksh*am*
tonight	bu gece	boo ghej*eh*
yesterday afternoon	dün öğleden sonra	d*ewn* ur-l*eden* s*o*nra
last night	dün gece	d*ewn* ghej*eh*
tomorrow morning	yarın sabah	yar*uhn* sab*ah*
tomorrow night	yarın gece	yar*uhn* ghej*eh*
in three days	üç gün sonra	ewch ghewn s*o*nra
three days ago	üç gün önce	ewch ghewn *urn*-jeh
late	geç	ghech
early	erken	erk*en*
soon	yakında	yak*uh*nda
later on	daha sonra	dah*a* s*o*nra
at the moment	şu anda	shoo *a*nda
second	saniye	sanee-y*eh*
minute	dakika	dak*ee*ka
ten minutes	on dakika	on dak*ee*ka
quarter of an hour	çeyrek saat	chay-r*ek* s*a*-at
half an hour	yarım saat	yar*uhm* s*a*-at
three quarters of an hour	kırk beş dakika	k*uh*rk besh dak*ee*ka
hour	saat	s*a*-at
day	gün	ghewn
week	hafta	haft*a*

15

TIME

fortnight	on beş gün	*on besh ghewn*
month	ay	*'eye'*
year	yıl	*yuhl*

TELLING THE TIME

The simplest way of telling the time in Turkish is by placing the minutes after the hour, e.g. 6.15 = 'altı on beş'; 9.40 = 'dokuz kırk'. Alternatively the same word order can be used with the addition of 'var' (to express 'to') or 'geçiyor' (to express 'past'): twenty to five = 'beşe yirmi var'; ten past eight = 'sekizi on geçiyor'. 'Buçuk' is used for half hours, as in 3.30 'üc buçuk'; the only exception being 12.30, 'yarım' (literally: half). The 24 hour clock is widely used, both in timetables and in writing, as well as verbally. There are no equivalents in Turkish to 'a.m.' or 'p.m.'.

one o'clock	saat bir	*sa-at beer*
ten past one	biri on geçiyor	*beeree on ghecheeyor*
quarter past one	biri çeyrek geçiyor	*beeree chay-rek ghecheeyor*
twenty past one	biri yirmi geçiyor	*beeree yeermee ghecheeyor*
half past one	bir buçuk	*beer boochook*
twenty to two	ikiye yirmi var	*eekee-yeh yeermee var*
quarter to two	ikiye çeyrek var	*eekee-yeh chay-rek var*
ten to two	ikiye on var	*eekee-yeh on var*
two o'clock	saat iki	*sa-at eekee*
13.00	saat on üç	*sa-at on ewch*
16.30	on altı otuz	*on altuh otooz*
20.10	yirmi on	*yeermee on*
at half past five	beş buçukta	*besh boochookta*
at seven o'clock	saat yedide	*sa-at yedeedeh*
noon	öğleyin	*urleh-yeen*
midnight	gece yarısı	*ghejeh yaruhssuh*

HOTELS

Turkish hotels follow the usual five-star classification ranging from 'Lüks' (5 star) to fourth class (1 star). Some hotels are certified by the government as 'tourist' hotels and such establishments are obliged to observe certain standards. Many others are monitored by local authorities. In addition to hotels, there are also motels, holiday villages called 'tatil köyü' (*tateel kur-yew*), self-catering apartments and rooms in private houses – 'pansiyon'. It's a good idea to have a look at the room before you take it and to check if the toilet and washbasin are in working order. Information about hotel accommodation may be obtained from Tourism and Information Bureaus.

USEFUL WORDS AND PHRASES

balcony	balkon	*balkon*
bathroom	banyo	*ban-yo*
bed	yatak	*yatak*
bedroom	yatak odası	*yatak odassuh*
bill	hesap	*hessap*
blanket	battaniye	*bat-tanee-yeh*
breakfast	kahvaltı	*kahvaltuh*
cold water	soğuk su	*so-ook soo*
dining room	yemek salonu	*yemek salonoo*
dinner	akşam yemeği	*aksham yemeh-ee*
double room	iki kişilik oda	*eekee keesheeleek oda*
foyer	giriş holü,	*gheereesh holew,*
	fuaye	*fw-'eye'-yeh*
full board	tam pansiyon	*tam pansseeyon*
half board	yarım pansiyon	*yaruhm pansseeyon*
hotel	otel	*otel*
hot water	sıcak su	*suhjak soo*
key	anahtar	*anahtar*
lift	asansör	*assanssur*

lounge	salon	*salon*
lunch	öğle yemeği	*ur-leh yemeh-ee*
manager	müdür	*mewdewr*
plug	tıkaç	*tuhkach*
receipt	makbuz	*makbooz*
reception	resepsiyon	*ressepsseeyon*
receptionist	resepsiyon görevlisi	*ressepsseeyon gurevleessee*
restaurant	lokanta, restoran	*lokanta, restoran*
room	oda	*oda*
room service	oda servisi	*oda serveessee*
shower	duş	*doosh*
single room	tek kişilik oda	*tek keesheeleek oda*
toilet	tuvalet	*toovalet*
toilet paper	tuvalet kağıdı	*toovalet ka-uhduh*
twin room	çift yataklı oda	*cheeft yatakluh oda*
washbasin	lavabo	*lavabo*

Have you any vacancies?
Boş odanız var mı?
bosh odanuhz var muh?

I have a reservation
Rezervasyonum var
rezervass-yonoom var

I'd like a single room
Tek kişilik bir oda istiyorum
tek keesheeleek beer oda eesteeyoroom

We'd like a double room
İki kişilik bir oda istiyoruz
eekee keesheeleek beer oda eesteeyorooz

Do you have a twin room?
Çift yataklı bir odanız var mı?
cheeft yataklúh beer odanúhz var muh?

I'd like a room with a bathroom/balcony
Banyolu/balkonlu bir oda istiyorum
ban-yoloo/balkonloo beer oda eesteeyoroom

I'd like a room for one night/three nights
Bir/üç gece için bir oda istiyorum
beer/ewch ghejeh eecheen beer oda eesteeyoroom

I don't know yet how long I'll stay
Ne kadar kalacağımı henüz bilmiyorum
neh kadar kalaja-uhmuh henewz beelmeeyoroom

19

What is the charge per night?
Bir gecelik ücreti ne kadar?
beer ghejeleek ewjretee neh kadar?

May I have a look at the room?
Odayı görebilir miyim?
od-'eye'-yuh gurebeeleer meeyeem?

When is breakfast/dinner?
Kahvaltı/akşam yemeği saat kaçta?
kahvaltuh/aksham yemeh-ee sa-at kachta?

Would you have my luggage brought up?
Lütfen bagajımı odama çıkartın
lewtfen bagajuhmuh odama chuhkartuhn

Please call me at ... o'clock
Lütfen beni saat ...-da uyandırın
lewtfen benee sa-at ...-da oo-yanduhruhn

Can I have breakfast in my room?
Odamda kahvaltı edebilir miyim?
odamda kahvaltuh edebeeleer meeyeem?

I'll be back at ... o'clock
Saat ...-de döneceğim
sa-at ...-deh durnejeh-eem

My room number is ...
... numarada kalıyorum
... noomarada kaluhyoroom

I'm leaving tomorrow
Yarın ayrılıyorum
yaruhn 'eye'-ruhluhyoroom

May I have my bill please?
Hesabımı rica ediyorum
hessabuhmuh reeja edeeyoroom

Can you recommend another hotel?
Başka bir otel tavsiye edebilir misiniz?
bashka beer otel tavssee-yeh edebeeleer mee-seeneez?

Can you get me a taxi?
Lüften bana bir taksi çağırır mısınız?
lewtfen bana beer takssee cha-uhruhr muh-suh-nuhz?

The toilet won't flush
Tuvalet tıkandı
toovalet tuhkanduh

There's no water
Su yok
soo yok

There's no plug in the washbasin
Lavaboda tıkaç yok
lavaboda tuhkach yok

THINGS YOU'LL SEE OR HEAR

akşam yemeği	dinner
asansör	lift, elevator
bagaj	luggage
balkon	balcony
banyo	bath
basın	press
çekin	pull
çift yataklı oda	twin room

⟶

çocuklar	children
dolu	full, no vacancies
duş	shower
gece	night
hesap	bill
iki kişilik oda	double room
kahvaltı	breakfast
kahvaltı dahil	breakfast included
kat	floor, storey
K.D.V.	VAT
komple kahvaltı	full breakfast
oda	room
öğle yemeği	lunch
pansiyon	bed in a private house (no breakfast)
resepsiyon	reception
rezervasyon	reservation
şofben	water heater
tam pansiyon	full board
tek kişilik oda	single room
tuvalet	toilet
yangın çıkışı	emergency exit
yarım pansiyon	half board
yemek salonu	dining room
zemin kat	ground floor

CAMPING AND CARAVANNING

In Turkey there are still not very many well-equipped and 'approved' camp or caravan sites, but adequate campsites, sometimes with private beaches, may be found on principal routes and at tourist centres. These are generally open from April or May until October. Camping on private ground away from official campsites requires the landlord's permission.

Some student hostels double as youth hostels during vacations.

USEFUL WORDS AND PHRASES

bucket	kova	*kova*
campfire	kamp ateşi	*kamp ateshee*
campsite	kamp yeri	*kamp yeree*
to go camping	kamp yapmak	*kamp yapmak*
caravan	karavan	*karavan*
caravan site	kamping	*kampeeng*
cooking utensils	kap kaçak	*kap kachak*
drinking water	içme suyu	*eechmeh soo-yoo*
ground sheet	su geçirmez yaygı	*soo ghech-eer-mez yay-guh*
guy rope	çadır ipi	*chaduhr eepee*
to hitch-hike	otostop yapmak	*otostop yapmak*
rope	ip	*eep*
rubbish	çöp	*churp*
rucksack	sırt çantası	*suhrt chantassuh*
saucepans	tencereler	*tenjereh-ler*
sleeping bag	uyku tulumu	*ooy-koo tooloomoo*
tent	çadır	*chaduhr*
youth hostel	gençlik yurdu	*ghench-leek yurdoo*

Can I camp here?
Burada kamp yapabilir miyim?
boorada kamp yapabeeleer mee-yeem?

CAMPING AND CARAVANNING

Can we park the caravan here?
Karavanı buraya park edebilir miyiz?
karavanuh boora-ya park edebeeleer mee-yeez?

Where is the nearest campsite/caravan site?
En yakın kamp yeri/kamping nerede?
en yakuhn kamp yeree/kampeeng neh-reh-deh?

What is the charge per night?
Bir gecelik ücreti kaç lira?
beer gheh-jeh-leek ewj-retee kach leera?

What facilities are there?
Ne gibi imkanlar var?
neh gheebee eemkanlar var?

Can I light a fire here?
Burada ateş yakabilir miyim?
boorada atesh yakabeeleer mee-yeem?

Where can I get ...?
Nerede ... bulabilirim?
neh-reh-deh ... boolabeeleereem?

Is there drinking water here?
Burada içme suyu var mı?
boorada eechmeh soo-yoo var muh?

THINGS YOU'LL SEE OR HEAR

ateş	fire
battaniye	blanket
çadır	tent
çadır bezi	tarpaulin
çadır direği	tent pole
çadır kazığı	tent peg
duş	shower
hela	toilet
ışık	light
içme suyu	drinking water
kamp ateşi	campfire
kamp yapmak yasaktır	no camping
kamp yeri	campsite
karavan	caravan
kimlik	identification
kira ücreti	hire charge
kullanım	use
mutfak	kitchen
römorkör	trailer
tuvalet	toilet
uyku tulumu	sleeping bag
ücretler	charges
yasak	not permitted
yasak bölge	restricted zone
yatakhane	dormitory

MOTORING

The national highway network mostly consists of single-lane asphalt roads which connect all major cities and towns. With the exception of the very busy main road between Istanbul and Ankara, which is inadequate, inter-city links are able to cope with the relatively low volume of traffic. There are short stretches of motorway ('ekspresyol') near Istanbul and at both ends of the Bosphorus Bridge, where a toll is charged. Secondary roads are fairly poor in quality and are mostly surfaced with gravel chippings.

The Turkish traffic code is similar to those in European countries, the rule being that you drive on the right and overtake on the left. International traffic signs are used. Traffic coming from the right has priority at crossroads and junctions wherever there are no priority signs or traffic lights.

In built-up areas a speed limit of 50 km/h (31 mph) is shown by a red-bordered circular sign with the number 50 in black. A similar black and white sign with black diagonal stripes signals the end of the speed limit. Outside built-up areas, the general speed limit is 99 km/h (61 mph).

All motorists entering Turkey by car from abroad should have a green card certificate of insurance. Your passport will be endorsed upon entry and this must be cancelled before you can leave the country.

There are plenty of petrol stations on main roads, and most of them stay open 24 hours. Many have restaurants and shops attached to them. Petrol is sold in two grades: 'süper' is 4-star, 'normal' is 2/3 star.

SOME COMMON ROAD SIGNS

azami genişlik	maximum width
azami hız	maximum speed
azami park 1 saat	parking limited to 1 hour
azami yükseklik	maximum height
çıkış	exit
çıkmaz sokak	cul-de-sac
daralan kaplama	road narrows
devamlı virajlar	series of bends
dikkat	caution
dönel kavşak	roundabout
dur	stop
durmak yasaktır	no stopping
durulmaz	no stopping
ekspresyolun sonu	end of motorway
geç	cross
geçme yasağı	no overtaking
geri dönülmez	no U-turns
gevşek malzeme	loose chippings
gevşek şev	falling rock
hemzemin geçit	level crossing
hız kısıtlaması sonu	end of speed restriction
iki yönlü trafik	two-way traffic
karşıdan gelen taşıtlara öncelik	oncoming traffic has right of way
kasis	uneven road surface
kavşak	junction
kaygan yol	slippery road
otopark	car park
park yapılmaz	no parking
sağa dönülmez	no right turn
sağa/sola viraj	bend to right/left
sağdan gidiniz	keep to the right

⟶

sert viraj	sharp bend
sola dönülmez	no left turn
tali yol kavşağı	crossroads
taşıt giremez	no entry for vehicles
taşıt trafiğine kapalı yol	closed to all vehicles
tehlikeli eğim	steep gradient
tek yönlü yol	one-way street
tren yolu geçidi	level crossing
viraj	bend
yavaş	drive slowly
yaya geçidi	pedestrian crossing
yolda çalışma	roadworks
yol kapalı	road closed
yol ver	give way

USEFUL WORDS AND PHRASES

automatic	otomatik	*otomateek*
boot	bagaj	*bagaj*
brake	fren	*fren*
breakdown	arıza	*aruhza*
car	otomobil, araba	*otomobeel, araba*
caravan	karavan	*karavan*
clutch	debriyaj	*debreeyaj*
crossroads	tali yol kavşağı	*talee yol kavsha-uh*
to drive	sürmek	*sewrmek*
engine	motor	*motor*
exhaust	egzoz	*egzoz*
fanbelt	vantilatör kayışı	*vanteelatur k-'eye'-yuhshuh*
garage	garaj	*garaj*
gear	vites	*veetess*
gears	vitesler	*veetessler*

gearbox	vites kutusu	*veetess kootoossoo*
junction *(motorway)*	kavşak	*kavshak*
licence	ehliyet	*ehleeyet*
lights *(head)*	farlar	*farlar*
(rear)	arka lambalar	*arka lambalar*
lorry	kamyon	*kam-yon*
manual	düz	*dewz*
mirror	ayna	*'eye'-na*
motorbike	motosiklet	*motoseeklet*
motorway	ekspresyol	*ekspress-yol*
number plate	plaka	*plaka*
petrol	benzin	*benzeen*
petrol station	benzin istasyonu	*benzeen eestass-yonoo*
road	yol	*yol*
skid	kayma	*k-'eye'-ma*
spares	yedek parçalar	*yedek parchalar*
speed	hız	*huhz*
speed limit	hız tahdidi	*huhz tahdeedee*
speedometer	kilometre saati	*keelometreh sa-atee*
steering wheel	direksiyon	*deereksseeyon*
to tow *(away)*	çekmek	*chekmek*
traffic lights	trafik ışıkları	*trafeek uhshuhk-laruh*
trailer	römork	*rurmork*
tyre	dışlastik	*duhsh-lasteek*
van	kamyonet	*kam-yonet*
wheel	tekerlek	*tekerlek*
windscreen	ön cam	*urn jam*
windscreen wiper	silecek	*seelejek*

I need some petrol
Biraz benzine ihtiyacım var
beeraz benzeeneh eehtee-yajuhm var

I need some oil
Biraz yağa ihtiyacım var
beeraz ya-a eehtee-yajuhm var

Fill her up please!
Lütfen depoyu doldurun!
lewtfen depo-yoo doldooroon!

I'd like 10 litres of petrol
Lütfen 10 litre benzin
lewtfen on leetreh benzeen

Would you check the tyres please?
Lütfen lastikleri kontrol eder misiniz?
lewtfen lasteekleree kontrol eder mee-seeneez?

Where is the nearest garage?
En yakın garaj nerede?
en yakuhn garaj neh-reh-deh?

How do I get to ...?
...-e nasıl gidebilirim?
...-eh nasuhl gheedebeeleereem?

Is this the road to ...?
... yolu bu mu?
... yoloo boo moo?

Where can I park?
Nereye park edebilirim?
neh-reh-yeh park edebeeleereem?

Can I park here?
Buraya park edebilir miyim?
boora-ya park edebeeleer mee-yeem?

I'd like to hire a car
Bir otomobil kiralamak istiyorum
beer otomobeel keeralamak eesteeyoroom

Is there a mileage charge?
Ayrıca kilometre ücreti var mı?
'eye'-ruhja keelometreh ewjretee var muh?

DIRECTIONS YOU MAY BE GIVEN

çok uzak	it's a long way
çok yakın	it's very near
doğru gidin	go straight on
dümdüz devam edin	straight on
geri gidin	go back
...-i geçin	go past the ...
ikinci yoldan sapın	take the second turning
ilk yoldan sapın	take the first turning
sağ	right
sağa dönün	turn right
sağdan birinci	first on the right
sol	left
sola dönün	turn left
soldan ikinci	second on the left

REPLIES YOU MAY BE GIVEN

Otomatik mi düz vitesli mi istersiniz?
Would you like an automatic or a manual?

Ehliyetinizi verin, lütfen
May I see your licence?

Do you do repairs?
Tamir işleri yapıyor musunuz?
tameer eeshleree yapuhyor moo-soonooz?

31

Can you repair the clutch?
Debriyajı tamir edebilir misiniz?
debree-yaj__uh__ tam__eer__ edebeel__eer__ mee-seen__eez__?

How long will it take?
Ne kadar sürer?
neh kad__ar__ sewr__er__?

There is something wrong with the engine
Motorda bir arıza var
motord__a__ beer __a__ruhza var

The engine is overheating
Motor fazla ısınıyor
mot__or__ f__a__zla uhsuhnuh-y__or__

The brakes are binding
Pedala basılınca frenler sıkışıyor
pedal__a__ basuhl__uh__nja frenl__er__ suhkuh-shuhy__or__

I need a new tyre
Yeni bir lastik lazım
yen__ee__ beer l__a__steek la-z__uh__m

THINGS YOU'LL SEE OR HEAR

benzin	petrol, fuel
benzin istasyonu	fuel/petrol station
benzin pompası	petrol pump
cam sileceği	windscreen wiper
çıkış	exit
ekspresyol	motorway
ekspresyol kavşağı	motorway junction

gaz vermek	to accelerate
harita	map
hava basıncı	air pressure
kasis	uneven road surface
kenar şeridi	hard shoulder
kontrol etmek	to check
köy yolu	country road
lastik basıncı	tyre pressure
normal	2/3 star
ön cam	windscreen, windshield
süper	4 star
tali yol kavşağı	crossroads
tamir etmek	to repair
taşıt kuyruğu	tailback
trafik tıkanıklığı	traffic jam
yağ	oil
yağ seviyesi	oil level
yan geçit	by-pass
yavaş vasıta şeridi	crawler lane
yedek depo	spare tank

RAIL AND COACH TRAVEL

Turkish State Railways (TCDD) connect most major cities but are not famous for their efficiency. The best trains to travel by are the 'ekspres' trains, especially those operating between Izmir, Ankara and Istanbul, which are usually first class only. Long distance trains have couchettes, sleeping cars and restaurant cars. There are discounts of 10% for students, 20% for return tickets and 30% for groups of more than 15 persons.

The extensive coach network covering all Turkish towns and cities provides a popular, faster and more efficient alternative to trains. Coaches are cheap and run at frequent intervals, both day and night.

The coaches are very comfortable and usually contain a mini fridge at the back with bottles of cold drinking water, 'içme suyu' (*eechmeh soo-yoo*), to which passengers are free to help themselves. It is also the custom for lemon cologne to be brought around and sprinkled on to passengers' cupped hands during the journey. On long-distance journeys stops are made and passengers can buy refreshments both outside or inside the coach from sellers of various types of food, the most famous of these being the 'simitçi' (*seemeetchee*) or 'simit' seller, usually a small boy balancing on his head a round tray of 'simit' – circular rings of bread covered with sesame seeds.

USEFUL WORDS AND PHRASES

booking office	bilet gişesi	*beelet ghee-shessee*
buffet	büfe	*bewfeh*
carriage	vagon	*vagon*
coach	otobüs	*otobewss*
coach terminal	otogar	*otogar*
communication cord	imdat freni	*eemdat frenee*
compartment	kompartıman	*kompartuhman*
connection	bağlantı, aktarma	*ba-lantuh, aktarma*

34

currency exchange	kambiyo	*kambeeyo*
dining car	vagon restoran	*vagon restoran*
driver	şoför	*shofur*
engine	lokomotif	*lokomoteef*
entrance	giriş	*gheereesh*
exit	çıkış	*chuh-kuhsh*
first class	birinci sınıf	*beereenjee suh-nuhf*
to get in	binmek	*been-mek*
to get out	inmek	*een-mek*
guard	kondüktör	*kondewk-tur*
indicator board	gösterge levhası	*gurster-gheh levhassuh*
left luggage	emanet	*emanet*
lost property	kayıp eşya	*k-'eye'-uhp esh-ya*
luggage locker	emanet kasası	*emanet kassassuh*
luggage rack	bagaj rafı	*bagaj rafuh*
luggage trolley	eşya arabası	*esh-ya arabassuh*
luggage van	bagaj vagonu	*bagaj vagonoo*
platform	peron	*peron*
rail	ray	*r-'eye'*
railway	demiryolu	*demeer-yoloo*
reserved seat	ayrılmış yer	*'eye'-ruhl-muhsh yer*
restaurant car	vagon restoran	*vagon restoran*
return ticket	gidiş dönüş bileti	*gheedeesh durnewsh beeletee*
second class	ikinci sınıf	*eekeenjee suh-nuhf*
single ticket	gidiş bileti	*gheedeesh beeletee*
sleeping car	yataklı vagon	*yatakluh vagon*
station	istasyon	*eestass-yon*
station master	gar şefi	*gar shefee*
ticket	bilet	*beelet*
ticket collector	kondüktör	*kondewk-tur*
timetable	tarife	*tareefeh*
tracks	raylar	*r-'eye'-lar*
train	tren	*tren*
waiting room	bekleme salonu	*beklemeh salonoo*
window	pencere	*penjereh*

When does the train for ... leave?
... treni saat kaçta kalkıyor?
... trenee sa-at kachta kalkuh-yor?

When does the train from ... arrive?
... treni saat kaçta varacak?
... trenee sa-at kachta varajak?

When is the next train to ...?
...-e bundan sonraki tren saat kaçta?
...-eh boondan sonrakee tren sa-at kachta?

When is the first train to ...?
...-e ilk tren saat kaçta?
...-eh eelk tren sa-at kachta?

When is the last train to ...?
...-e son tren saat kaçta?
...-eh son tren sa-at kachta?

What is the fare to ...?
...-ya bir bilet kaç lira?
...-ya beer beelet kach leera?

Do I have to change?
Aktarma yapmam lazım mı?
aktarma yapmam la-zuhm muh?

Does the train stop at ...?
Tren ...-de duruyor mu?
tren ...-deh doorooyor moo?

How long does it take to get from ... to ...?
...-den ...-e kadar yol ne kadar sürer?
...-den ...-eh kadar yol neh kadar sewrer?

A single/return ticket to ... please
Lütfen, ...-e bir gidiş/gidiş dönüş bileti
lewtfen, ...-eh beer gheedeesh/gheedeesh durnewsh beeletee

Do I have to pay a supplement?
Fark ödemem gerekiyor mu?
fark urdemem gherekeeyor moo?

I'd like to reserve a seat
Bir yer ayırtmak istiyorum
beer yer 'eye'-uhrt-mak eesteeyoroom

Is this the right train for ...?
Bu ... treni midir?
boo ... trenee meedeer?

Is this the right platform for the ... train?
... treni bu perondan mı kalkıyor?
... trenee boo perondan muh kalkuh-yor?

Which platform for the ... train?
... treni hangi perondan kalkıyor?
... trenee hanghee perondan kalkuh-yor?

Is the train late?
Tren gecikti mi?
tren ghejeektee mee?

Could you help me with my luggage please?
Lütfen eşyalarımı taşımama yardım eder misiniz?
lewtfen esh-yalaruhmuh tashuh-mama yarduhm eder mee-seeneez?

Is this a non-smoking compartment?
Bu kompartıman sigara içmeyenleremu mahsus dur?
boo kompartuhman seegara eechmayenlerehmoo mah-sooss door?

RAIL TRAVEL

Is this seat free?
Bu yer boş mu?
boo yer bosh moo?

This seat is taken
Bu yerin sahibi var
boo yereen saheebee var

I have reserved this seat
Bu yeri ben ayırttım
boo yeree ben 'eye'-uhrt-tuhm

May I open/close the window?
Pencereyi açabilir/kapatabilir miyim?
penjereh-yee acha-beeleer/kapata-beeleer mee-yeem?

When do we arrive in ...?
...-e ne zaman varıyoruz?
...-eh neh zaman varuh-yorooz?

What station is this?
Bu istasyonun adı nedir?
boo eestass-yonoon aduh nedeer?

When does my connection leave?
Aktarma yapacağım tren kaçta kalkıyor?
aktarma yapaja-uhm tren kachta kalkuh-yor?

Do we stop at ...?
...-de duruyor muyuz?
...-deh doorooyor moo-yooz?

Would you keep an eye on my things for a moment?
Lütfen biraz eşyalarıma göz kulak olur musunuz?
lewtfen beeraz esh-yalaruhma gurz koolak oloor moo-soonooz?

Is there a restaurant car on this train?
Bu trende vagon restoran var mı?
boo trendeh vagon restoran var muh?

THINGS YOU'LL SEE OR HEAR

aktarma yapınız	change
ayrılmış yer	reserved seat
bekleme salonu	waiting room
bilet farkı	fare supplement
biletler	tickets
bilet otomatı	ticket machine
bininiz	get on board
boş	vacant
büfe	fast-food counter
Cumartesileri	Saturdays
çıkılmaz	no exit
çıkış	exit
...-de durmaz	does not stop at ...
dışarı sarkmayınız	do not lean out
dikkat	attention
ekspres	express
ekspres farkı	express train supplement
emanet	left luggage
emanet kasaları	luggage lockers
enformasyon	information
gecikme	delay
giriş	entry
... günleri dışında	... days excepted
güzergah	route
imdat freni	emergency cord
ininiz	get off/out
kalkış	departure
kambiyo	currency exchange
kapıları kapatınız	close the doors
kuşet	sleepers

→

39

merkez istasyonu	central station
meşgul	engaged
otobüs	coach
otogar	coach station
Pazar ve tatil günleri	Sundays and holidays
peron	platform
rötar	delay
seyahat	journey
seyahat hakkında bilgi	travel information
sigara içenler	smokers
sigara içmeyenler	non-smokers
şoför	driver
tarife	timetable
tatil	holidays
tuvalet	toilet
vagon	carriage, car
vagon restoran	restaurant car
varış	arrival
yalnız ... günleri	... days only
yataklı vagon	sleeping car
yer ayırtma	seat reservation

Tren ...-den kalkmak üzeredir
The train is about to depart from ...

Bir sonraki tren saat ...-dadır
The next train is at ...

Yalnız birinci sınıf bilet var
There are only first-class seats

...-de aktarma yapmanız gerekir
You have to change at ...

Fark ödeyeceksiniz
You must pay a supplement

Tren rötarlı
The train is late

AIR TRAVEL

Turkish Airlines (THY) operate scheduled flights to all major cities in the country. Flights between Izmir, Ankara and Istanbul are fairly frequent. There are discounts for students, children and sports groups. There are also private airlines which provide domestic flights between various regions but details of these are not always available outside Turkey.

USEFUL WORDS AND PHRASES

air hostess	hostes	*host<u>e</u>ss*
airline	havayolu	*hava-yol<u>oo</u>*
airport	havalimanı	*havaleeman<u>uh</u>*
airport bus	havalimanı otobüsü	*havaleeman<u>uh</u> otobewss<u>ew</u>*
aisle	koridor	*kore<u>e</u>dor*
arrival	varış	*var<u>uh</u>sh*
baggage claim	bagaj alma yeri	*bag<u>aj</u> alma yer<u>ee</u>*
boarding card	biniş kartı	*been<u>ee</u>sh kart<u>uh</u>*
check-in	bagaj kaydı	*bag<u>aj</u> k-'eye'-d<u>uh</u>*
check-in desk	bagaj kayıt masası	*bag<u>aj</u> k-'eye'-<u>uht</u> massass<u>uh</u>*
customs	gümrük	*ghewmr<u>e</u>wk*
delay	gecikme	*ghejeekm<u>e</u>h*
departure	kalkış	*kalk<u>uh</u>sh*
departure lounge	giden yolcular salonu	*ghe<u>e</u>den yoljool<u>a</u>r salon<u>oo</u>*
emergency exit	imdat çıkışı	*eemd<u>a</u>t chuh-k<u>uh</u>shuh*
flight	sefer	*sef<u>e</u>r*
flight number	sefer numarası	*sef<u>e</u>r noomarass<u>uh</u>*
gate	çıkış kapısı	*chuh-k<u>uh</u>sh kapuh-s<u>uh</u>*
jet	jet	*jet*
to land	inmek	*eenm<u>e</u>k*
passport	pasaport	*passap<u>o</u>rt*

41

passport control	pasaport kontrolü	*passaport kontrolew*
pilot	pilot	*peelot*
plane	uçak	*oochak*
runway	pist	*peest*
seat	koltuk	*koltook*
seat belt	emniyet kemeri	*emneeyet kemeree*
steward	kabin memuru	*kabeen memooroo*
stewardess	hostes	*hostess*
to take off	kalkmak	*kalkmak*
window	pencere	*penjereh*
wing	kanat	*kanat*

When is there a flight to ...?
...-ye ne zaman uçak var?
...-yeh neh zaman oochak var?

What time does the flight to ... leave?
... uçağı saat kaçta kalkıyor?
... oocha-uh sa-at kachta kalkuh-yor?

Is it a direct flight?
Direkt sefer midir?
deerekt sefer meedeer?

Do I have to change planes?
Uçak değiştirmem gerekiyor mu?
oochak deh-eeshteermem gherekeeyor moo?

When do I have to check in?
Bagajımı ne zaman vermem gerekiyor?
bagajuhmuh neh zaman vermem gherekeeyor?

I'd like a single/return ticket to ...
... bir gidiş/gidiş dönüş bileti istiyorum
... beer gheedeesh/gheedeesh durnewsh beeletee eesteeyoroom

I'd like a non-smoking seat please
Lütfen, sigara içilmeyen kısımdan bir yer verin
lewtfen, seegara eecheelmayen kuhsuhmdan beer yer vereen

I'd like a smoking seat please
Lütfen, sigara içilen kısımdan bir yer verin
lewtfen, seegara eecheelen kuhsuhmdan beer yer vereen

I'd like a window seat please
Lütfen, pencere yanından bir yer verin
lewtfen, penjereh yanuhndan beer yer vereen

How long will the flight be delayed?
Uçak ne kadar gecikecek?
oochak neh kadar ghejeekeh-jek?

Is this the right gate for the ... flight?
... uçağı için çıkış kapısı bu mudur?
... oocha-uh eecheen chuh-kuhsh kapuh-suh boo moodoor?

When do we arrive in ...?
...-ye saat kaçta varacağız?
...-yeh sa-at kachta varaja-uhz?

May I smoke now?
Şimdi sigara içebilir miyim?
sheemdee seegara eecheh-beeleer mee-yeem?

THINGS YOU'LL SEE OR HEAR

ara durak	intermediate stop
bagaj alma yeri	baggage claim
bagaj kaydı	check-in
bagaj kaydını yaptırınız	check in

⟶

43

bagaj kayıt masası	check-in desk
bagaj kontrolü	baggage check
çek-in	check-in
çıkış kapısı	gate
danışma	information
direkt sefer	direct flight
el bagajı	hand luggage
emniyet kemerlerinizi bağlayınız	fasten seat belts
enformasyon	information
gecikme	delay
gümrük	customs
hareket	departure
imdat çıkışı	emergency exit
iniş	landing
irtifa	altitude
mecburi iniş	emergency landing
pasaport kontrolü	passport control
sefer	flight
sigara içenler	smokers
sigara içilmez	no smoking
sigara içmeyenler	non-smokers
sigara içmeyiniz	refrain from smoking
tarifeli sefer	scheduled flight
uçak	aircraft
uçuşa hazır	ready for take-off
uçuş hızı	flight speed
uçuş süresi	flight time
varış	arrival
yerel saat	local time
yolcular	passengers

BY BUS, TAXI AND BOAT

Major Turkish cities and towns have bus networks which, though cheap, are generally crowded. Most work on a ticket system which requires a ticket or a book of tickets to be bought beforehand from a ticket kiosk. Private minibus and coach services also operate within big cities, particularly during the rush hour.

In large cities such as Istanbul, Ankara and Izmir, the overworked bus services are supplemented by 'dolmuş' (*dolmoosh*), a system of shared taxis, often capable of carrying 8-10 passengers. These operate between fixed destinations, but the passenger can get in and out at stops en route and pays according to the distance travelled. 'Dolmuş', which are usually recognizable by a yellow strip around them, are more expensive than buses but cheaper than taxis.

Taxis are numerous throughout Turkey and are distinguished by chequered black and yellow bands. Taximeters are generally fitted. Taxis may at times operate as 'dolmuş'.

The only underground in Turkey is a tiny train called 'Tünel' in Istanbul, running between Karaköy and Galatasaray. Tokens are bought at the 'token office' before passing through the turnstile.

In Istanbul boats 'vapur' (*vapoor*) provide public transport to various locations on both sides of the Bosphorus and the Princes' Islands. The popular tour which zig-zags up the Bosphorus is well worth trying.

There are also larger boats which provide regular services for travelling to the ports along the Black Sea, the Marmara and to the Aegean and Mediterranean coasts.

USEFUL WORDS AND PHRASES

adult	yetişkin	*yeteesh-keen*
boat	vapur	*vapoor*
book of tickets	küpür bilet	*kewpewr beelet*
bus	otobüs	*otobewss*
bus station	otobüs garajı, otogar	*otobewss garajuh, otogar*
bus stop	otobüs durağı	*otobewss doora-uh*
child	çocuk	*chojook*
coach	otobüs	*otobewss*
conductor	biletçi	*beelet-chee*
connection	bağlantı	*ba-lantuh*
cruise	vapur gezisi	*vapoor ghezeessee*
driver	şoför	*shofur*
fare	ücret	*ewj-ret*
ferry	araba vapuru	*araba vapooroo*
lake	göl	*gurl*
number 5 bus	5 numaralı otobüs	*besh numaraluh otobewss*
passenger	yolcu	*yoljoo*
port	liman	*leeman*
quay	iskele	*eess-keleh*
river	nehir	*neheer*
sea	deniz	*deneez*
seat	yer	*yer*
ship	gemi	*ghemee*
station	istasyon	*eestass-yon*
taxi	taksi	*taksee*
terminus	son durak	*son doorak*
ticket	bilet	*beelet*

Where is the bus station?
Otogar nerede?
otogar neh-reh-deh?

Where is there a bus stop?
Nerede otobüs durağı var?
neh-reh-deh otobewss doora-uh var?

Which buses go to ...?
Hangi otobüsler ...-e gider?
hanghee otobewss-ler ...-eh gheedeer?

How often do the buses to ... run?
...-e giden otobüslerin arası ne kadardır?
...-eh gheeden otobewss-lereen arassuh neh kadar-duhr?

Could you tell me when we get to ...?
...-e varınca bana haber verir misiniz?
...-ch varuhn-ja bana haber vereer mee-seeneez?

Do I have to get off yet?
İneceğim yere geldik mi?
eencjeh-eem yereh gheldeek mee?

How do you get to ... from here?
Buradan ...-e nasıl gidilir?
booradan ...-eh nassuhl gheedeeleer?

Is it very far?
Çok uzak mı?
chok oozak muh?

I want to go to ...
...-e gitmek istiyorum
...-eh gheet-mek eesteeyoroom

Do you go near ...?
... yakınından geçiyor musunuz?
... yakuhn-uhndan ghecheeyor moo-soonooz?

BY BUS, TAXI AND BOAT

Where can I buy a ticket?
Nereden bilet alabilirim?
neh-reh-den beelet ala-beeleereem?

Please close/open the window
Lütfen, pencereyi açın/kapayın
lewtfen, penjereh-yee achuhn/kap-'eye'-yuhn

Could you help me get a ticket?
Bilet almama yardım eder misiniz?
beelet almama yarduhm eder mee-seeneez?

When does the last bus leave?
Son otobüs saat kaçta kalkıyor?
son otobewss sa-at kachta kalkuh-yor?

THINGS YOU'LL SEE OR HEAR

abone kartı	season ticket
aylık bilet	monthly season ticket
banliyö tren şebekesi	local railway system
bilet	ticket
bozuk para	change
çıkış	exit
değiştirmek	to change
dolmuş	collective taxi
dolmuş durağı	collective taxi stand
duracak yer	standing room
durak	stop
gidiş dönüş bileti	return ticket
girilmez	no entry
giriş	entry
gösteriniz	show
günlük bilet	day ticket

haftalık bilet	weekly ticket
imdat çıkışı	emergency exit
imdat freni	emergency brake
iskele	boarding/landing pier
istasyon	station
kalkış	departure
kısa yolculuk	short journey
kontrolör	inspector
minibüs	minibus
otobüs garajı, otogar	bus station
otobüs/tren bileti	bus/train ticket
oturacak yer	seat
ödeyiniz	pay
öğrenci kartı	student's pass
önden/arkadan binilir	entry at front/back
özürlü kişiler	handicapped people
ray	track
sigara içmek yasaktır	no smoking
son durak	terminus
şoför	driver
tam ücret	exact fare
tek	single
Tünel	Istanbul underground
vapur	passenger ferry
varış	arrival
yalnız gidiş	single journey
yetişkinler	adults

RESTAURANTS

There is a good choice of restaurants – 'lokanta' – for the tourist who wishes to sample Turkish food. These range from expensive establishments to humble eating places offering a limited number of dishes. Not all restaurants will have a menu. If there is no menu the restaurant will rely on the waiter to tell the customers what is available or to invite them through to the kitchen to have a look at the dishes. There are also restaurants which specialize in certain types of food:

'Kebapçı' (*kebap-chuh*):
These are meat restaurants which the vegetarian would be well-advised to avoid. The meat, mostly lamb, is grilled or barbecued in various ways and eaten with salads. They feature regional varieties such as 'Urfa Kebabı' (*oorfa kebabuh*) – very hot, or 'Bursa Kebabı' (*boorsa kebabuh*) – mild.

'Balık Lokantası' (*baluhk lokantassuh*):
Fish restaurants which can be found at port cities, and especially along the Bosphorus in Istanbul. They merit a visit not only for the fresh sea-food and the rich selection of hors d'oeuvre ('meze') which they serve, but also for the general merriment that results from the 'rakı' (*rakuh*) traditionally drunk with such food.

'İşkembeci' (*eesh-kembejee*):
The Turkish equivalent of the fish and chip shop, offering cheap and nourishing food. However, they are definitely not for the faint-hearted as they specialize in all types of offal and excel in tripe soup which gives them their name.

'Muhallebici' (*muhal-lebeejee*):
This is usually a clean, pleasant place serving a rich variety of puddings. They also offer a clear chicken soup and chicken and rice, and are therefore used by the Turks for a light lunch.

'Kahve' (*kahveh*) or 'kahvehane' (*kahveh-haneh*):
This is a coffee-shop where traditionally men sit playing 'tavla' (backgammon) and drinking tea, coffee and soft drinks. The 'çayhane' (*ch-'eye'-haneh*) is a more suitable place for families. There are usually tables and chairs outside where you can sit and buy tea – by the cup or by the samovar, 'semaver' (*semaver*). You can also have coffee or soft drinks and will be allowed to eat your own food.

Finally, a host of restaurants on pushcarts, some quite elaborate affairs, which serve mainly one type of food and congregate at crowded spots. Although their offerings may be quite tasty, their standards of hygiene are the subject of many jokes among the Turks and you should consider the risk before venturing to try them.

USEFUL WORDS AND PHRASES

beer	bira	*beera*
bill	hesap	*hessap*
bottle	şişe	*sheesheh*
bowl	kase	*ka-seh*
cake	pasta	*pasta*
chef	şef, ahçı	*shef, ah-chuh*
coffee	kahve	*kah-veh*
cup	fincan	*feenjan*
fork	çatal	*chatal*
glass	bardak	*bardak*
knife	bıçak	*buh-chak*
menu	yemek listesi	*yemek leestessee*
milk	süt	*sewt*
plate	tabak	*tabak*
receipt	makbuz	*makbooz*
sandwich	sandviç	*sand-veech*
serviette	peçete	*pecheteh*
snack	hafif yemek	*hafeef yemek*

RESTAURANTS

soup	çorba	*chorba*
spoon	kaşık	*kashuhk*
sugar	şeker	*sheker*
table	masa	*massa*
tea	çay	*ch-'eye'*
teaspoon	çay kaşığı	*ch-'eye' kassuh-uh*
tip	bahşiş	*bah-sheesh*
waiter/waitress	garson	*garson*
water	su	*soo*
wine	şarap	*sharap*
wine list	şarap listesi	*sharap leesteesee*

A table for 1/2 please
1/2 kişilik bir masa, lütfen
beer/eekee keeshee-leek beer massa, lewtfen

Can we see the menu/wine list?
Yemek/şarap listesini görebilir miyiz?
yemek/sharap leestesseenee gureh-beeleer mee-yeez?

What would you recommend?
Ne tavsiye edersiniz?
neh tav-see-yeh eder-seeneez?

I'd like ...
... istiyorum
... cesteeyoroom

Just a cup of coffee, please
Yalnız bir fincan kahve, lütfen
yalnuhz beer feenjan kah-veh, lewtfen

Waiter/waitress!
Garson!
garson!

Can we have the bill, please?
Hesabı getirir misiniz, lütfen?
hessabuh gheeteereer mee-seeneez, lewtfen?

I only want a snack
Yalnız hafif bir şey istiyorum
yalnuhz hafeef beer shay eesteeyoroom

Is there a set menu?
Tabldot var mı?
tabldot var muh?

I didn't order this
Ben bunu ısmarlamadım
ben boonoo uhss-marlamaduhm

May we have some more ...?
Biraz daha ... rica ediyoruz
beeraz daha ... reeja edeeyorooz

The meal was very good, thank you
Yemek çok iyiydi, teşekkür ederiz
yemek chok ee-yee-dee, teshek-kewr edereez

My compliments to the chef!
Ahçınızın eline sağlık!
ah-chuhnuhzuhn eleeneh sa-luhk!

YOU MAY HEAR

Afiyet olsun!
Enjoy your meal

MENU GUIDE

Adana kebabı	spicy hot meatballs
ahududu	raspberries
alabalık	trout
ananas	pineapple
ançüvez	anchovies
armut	pears
Arnavut ciğeri	'Albanian' spicy fried liver with onions
aşure	'Noah's pudding' – a dessert with wheat grains, nuts and dried fruit
ayran	yoghurt drink
ayva	quince
ayva laabı	quince jelly
ayva reçeli	quince jam
az pişmiş	rare
az şekerli kahve	slightly sweetened Turkish coffee
badem	almonds
badem kurabiyesi	almond cakes
badempare	almond cakes in syrup
badem tatlısı	almond cakes
bakla	broad beans
baklava	pastry filled with nuts and syrup
bal	honey
balık	fish
balık buğulaması	fish baked with tomatoes
balık çorbası	fish and lemon soup
balık kızartması	fried fish
balık köftesi	fish balls
bamya	okra
barbunya	red mullet
barbunya pilakisi	dried beans cooked in olive oil and served hot or cold
barbunya tava	fried red mullet
bazlama	flat bread cooked on a hot-plate
beyaz peynir	white cheese
beyaz peynirli makarna	noodles with white cheese
beyaz şarap	white wine
beyin salatası	brain salad
bezelye	green peas

bıldırcın	quail
biber	peppers
biber dolması	stuffed green peppers
biftek	steak
bira	beer
bisküvi	biscuits
bonfile	fillet steak
boza	thick fermented grain drink
böbrek	kidneys
böbrek ızgara	grilled kidneys
böbrek sote	sautéed kidneys
börek	layered pastry with cheese/meat/ spinach filling
buğulama	steamed, poached
bulgur pilavı	cracked wheat cooked with tomatoes
Bursa kebabı	grilled lamb on pitta bread with tomato sauce and yoghurt
buz	ice
buzlu	with ice
bülbül yuvası	dessert with nuts and syrup
cacık	chopped cucumber in garlic-flavoured yoghurt
ceviz	walnuts
ciğer	liver
ciğer sarması	minced liver wrapped in lamb's fat
ciğer tava	fried liver
cin	gin
cintonik	gin and tonic
çam fıstığı	pine nuts
çavdar ekmeği	rye bread
çay	tea
Çerkez tavuğu	'Circassian' cold chicken in walnut sauce with garlic
çılbır	poached eggs with yoghurt
çiğ köfte	raw meatballs: a dish made of minced meat, pounded wheat and chilli powder
çikolata	chocolate
çikolatalı	with chocolate
çikolatalı dondurma	chocolate ice cream
çikolatalı pasta	chocolate cake

çilek	strawberry
çilekli dondurma	strawberry ice cream
çilek reçeli	strawberry jam
çips	crisps
çiroz	salted dried mackerel
çoban salatası	mixed tomatoes, peppers, cucumbers and onion salad
çok pişmiş	well-done
çok şekerli kahve	very sweet Turkish coffee
çorba	soup
çöp kebabı	small pieces of lamb baked on wooden spits
çörek	kind of bun
çulluk	woodcock
dana eti	veal
dana rozbif	roast veal
deniz ürünleri	seafood
dereotu	dill
dil	ox tongue
dil balığı	sole
dilber dudağı	lip-shaped sweet pastry with nut filling
dolma	stuffed vegetables (with or without meat)
domates	tomatoes
domatesli	with tomatoes
domatesli pilav	rice cooked with tomatoes
domatesli pirinç çorbası	rice and tomato soup
domates salatası	tomato salad
domates salçalı patlıcan kızartması	fried aubergines with tomato and garlic sauce
domates salçası	tomato sauce
domates suyu	tomato juice
dondurma	ice cream
döner kebab	lamb grilled on a spit and served in thin slices, usually served with rice and salad
dut	mulberries
düğün çorbası	'wedding' soup made of meat stock, yoghurt and egg
ekmek	bread

ekmek kadayıfı	sweet pastry
ekşi	sour
elma	apples
elma suyu	apple juice
elma tatlısı	dessert made with apples
enginar	artichokes
erik	plums
erişte	homemade noodles
et	meat
etli	with meat
etli Ayşe kadın	meat with green beans
etli bezelye	pea stew
etli biber dolması	peppers stuffed with rice and meat
etli bulgur pilavı	cracked wheat with meat
etli domates dolması	tomatoes stuffed with meat and rice
etli kabak dolması	marrows stuffed with meat and rice
etli kapuska	cabbage stew with meat
etli kuru fasulye	lamb and haricot beans in tomato sauce
etli lahana dolması	cabbage leaves stuffed with meat and rice
etli nohut	chickpea and meat stew
etli yaprak dolması	vine leaves stuffed with rice and meat
et suyu	meat stock
ezme(si)	purée
ezo gelin çorbası	lentil and rice soup
fasulye	beans
fasulye pilaki	beans in olive oil
fasulye piyazı	beans and onion salad
fava	broad bean purée
fındık	hazelnuts
fırın	baked, oven-roasted
fırında	baked, oven-roasted
fıstık	pistachio nuts
fıstıklı	with pistachio nuts
fıstıklı dondurma	ice cream with pistachio nuts
fıstıklı muhallebi	rice flour and rosewater pudding with pistachio nuts
füme	smoked
gazoz	fizzy drink

greyfurut	grapefruit
güllaç	rice wafers stuffed with nuts, cooked in milk
gümüş	silverfish
güveç	meat and vegetable stew
güvercin	pigeon
hamsi	anchovy
hanım parmağı	'Lady's Fingers - dried dough sticks in syrup
hardal	mustard
haşlama	boiled, stewed
haşlanmış yumurta	boiled egg
havuç	carrots
havuç salatası	shredded carrot salad
havyar	caviar
hazır yemek	ready-to-eat food
helva	general name for various sweets made from cereals, nuts, sesame oil and honey
hıyar	cucumber
hindi	turkey
hindiba	wild chicory
hindi dolması	stuffed turkey
hindistan cevizi	coconut
hoşaf	stewed fruit
hurma	dates
hünkar beğendi	'Sultan's Delight' - lamb served with aubergine purée
ıhlamur	lime blossom tea
ıspanak	spinach
ıspanaklı börek	spinach wrapped in thin pastry
ıspanaklı yumurta	eggs with spinach
ızgara	grilled
ızgara balık	grilled fish
ızgara köfte	grilled meatballs
içecek	beverage
içki	alcoholic drink
içli köfte	meatballs stuffed with cracked wheat
iç pilav	rice with currrants, pine nuts and onions
imam bayıldı	split aubergines with tomatoes and

	onions, eaten cold with olive oil
incir	figs
irmik helvası	semolina 'helva'
İskender kebabı	grilled lamb on pitta bread with tomato sauce and yoghurt
islim kebabı	steamed kebab
istakoz	lobster
istiridye	oysters
işkembe çorbası	tripe soup
iyi pişmiş	well-done, well-cooked
jambon	ham
kabak	courgettes, pumpkin, marrow
kabak dolması	stuffed courgettes
kabak kızartması	fried marrows
kabak reçeli	marrow jam
kabak tatlısı	pumpkin with syrup and walnuts
kadın budu köfte	'Lady's Thighs' – meat and rice croquettes
kadın göbeği	'Lady's Navel' – flour and egg-based fried dessert soaked in syrup
kağıt kebabı	lamb and vegetables in paper
kağıtta barbunya	red mullet grilled in paper wrapping
kağıtta pişmiş	baked in paper
kahve	coffee
kakao	cocoa
kalkan	turbot
kanyak	brandy
kara biber	black pepper
karadut	black mulberries
karagöz	black bream
kara zeytin	black olives
karışık	mixed
karışık dondurma	mixed ice cream
karışık ızgara	mixed grill
karışık salata	mixed salad
karides	prawns
karides tavası	prawns fried in batter
karnabahar	cauliflower
karnabahar tavası	fried cauliflower
karnıyarık	split aubergines with meat filling
karpuz	water melon

kaşar peyniri	mild yellow cheese
kaşar peynirli makarna	noodles with 'kaşar' cheese
kavun	honeydew melon
kavunlu dondurma	melon ice cream
kayısı	apricots
kayısı reçeli	apricot jam
kayısı suyu	apricot juice
kaymak	clotted cream
kaymaklı	with clotted cream
kaymaklı dondurma	dairy ice cream
kaz	goose
kazan dibi	pudding with a caramel base
kebap	roast meat
kefal	grey mullet
kefal pilakisi	mullet cooked in olive oil with vegetables
kek	cake
keklik	partridge
kereviz	celery
kestane	chestnuts
kestane şekeri	marrons glacés, candied chestnuts
keşkek	lamb with wheat
keşkül	almond pudding
kılıç (balığı)	swordfish
kılıç ızgara	grilled swordfish
kılıç şiş	swordfish on skewers
kırmızı biber	paprika
kırmızı mercimek çorbası	red lentil soup
kırmızı şarap	red wine
kısır	cracked wheat and paprika
kış türlüsü	stewed winter vegetables
kıyma	minced meat
kıymalı	with minced meat
kıymalı bamya	okra with minced meat
kıymalı ıspanak	spinach with minced meat
kıymalı karnabahar	cauliflower with minced meat
kıymalı makarna	noodles with minced meat
kıymalı mercimek	meat and lentils
kıymalı pide	pitta bread with meat filling
kıymalı yumurta	eggs with minced meat
kızarmış ekmek	toast

kızartma	fried, broiled
kiraz	cherries
koç yumurtası	'ram's eggs' – a delicacy made from ram's testicles
kokoreç	lamb's intestines grilled on a spit
komposto	cold stewed fruit
koyun eti	mutton
köfte	meatballs or patties
köpüklü şarap	sparkling wine
krema	cream
kremalı pasta	cream cake
krem karamel	crème caramel
kurabiye	cake with almonds or nuts
kuru	dried
kuru fasulye	haricot beans in tomato sauce
kuru köfte	fried meatballs
kuru üzüm	raisins
kuru yemiş	dried fruit and nuts
kuskus pilavı	cous-cous – cooked semolina, usually served with meat
kuşbaşı	small pieces of casseroled meat
kuşkonmaz	asparagus
kuzu eti	lamb
kuzu fırında	roast leg of lamb
kuzu kapama	lamb with lettuce
kuzu pirzolası	grilled lamb chops
lahana	cabbage
lahana dolması	stuffed cabbage leaves
lahana turşusu	pickled cabbage
lahmacun	pancakes with spicy meat filling
leblebi	small chickpeas
levrek	sea bass
likör	liqueur
limon	lemon
limonata	still lemon drink
limonlu dondurma	lemon ice cream
lokum	Turkish Delight
lüfer	bluefish
maden suyu	mineral water
makarna	macaroni, noodles
mandalina	tangerines

MENU GUIDE

mantar	mushrooms
mantı	type of ravioli
marmelat	jam
marul	lettuce
maydanoz	parsley
mayonezli balık	fish with mayonnaise
menba suyu	spring water
menemen	omelette with tomatoes and peppers
mercan	bream
mercimek	lentils
mercimek çorbası	lentil soup
mersin balığı	sturgeon
meşrubat	soft drinks
meyva suyu	fruit juice
meze	hors d'oeuvres
mısır	corn
midye	mussels
midye dolması	stuffed mussels
midyeli pilav	rice with mussels
midye pilakisi	mussels cooked in oil with vegetables
midye tavası	fried mussels
muhallebi	rice flour and rosewater pudding
musakka	moussaka
muska böreği	triangles of pastry filled with cheese, parsley etc
muz	banana
mücver	vegetable patties
nane	mint
nar	pomegranate
nemse böreği	meat pie with puff pastry
neskafe	any brand of instant coffee
nohut	cooked chickpeas
nohutlu paça	lamb's trotters with chickpeas
nohutlu yahni	lamb and chickpeas
omlet	omelette
orta pişmiş	medium
orta şekerli kahve	medium sweet Turkish coffee
ördek	duck
paça	lamb's trotters
paça çorbası	lamb's trotter soup
palamut	tunny

pancar	beetroot
pancar turşusu	pickled beetroot
papatya çayı	camomile tea
paskalya çöreği	Easter bread - slightly sweetened bread in a plaited shape
pasta	cake
pastırma	cummin and garlic cured beef
pastırmalı yumurta	fried eggs with 'pastırma'
patates	potatoes
patates köftesi	potato and cheese balls
patates kızartması	chips
patatesli	with potatoes
patates püresi	creamed potatoes
patates salatası	potato salad
patlıcan	aubergines
patlıcan dolma turşusu	pickled stuffed aubergines
patlıcan kebabı	aubergine wrapped around pieces of meat and roasted
patlıcan kızartması	fried aubergines
patlıcanlı pilav	rice with aubergines
patlıcan salatası	aubergine purée
pavurya	crab
pembe şarap	rosé wine
peynir	cheese
peynirli	with cheese
peynirli omlet	cheese omelette
peynirli pide	cheese pitta bread
peynirli tepsi böreği	cheese pie
peynir tatlısı	small cheese cakes in syrup
pırasa	leek
pide	pitta bread
pilaki	cold white beans vinaigrette
pilav	rice cooked in butter
pilavlı tavuk	chicken and rice
piliç	chicken
piliç ızgarası	grilled chicken
pirinç	rice (uncooked)
pirzola	lamb chops
pisi	plaice
pişkin	well-cooked
piyaz	haricot bean salad

poğaça	pastries with meat or cheese filling
portakal	oranges
portakal reçeli	orange jam
portakal suyu	orange juice
puf böreği	meat or cheese pasties
püre	purée
rafadan	soft-boiled egg
rakı	Turkish national drink - distilled from grape juice and aniseed-flavoured
reçel	jam
revani	sweet semolina pastry
roka	kind of watercress
rom	rum
rosto	roasted
rus salatası	Russian salad - mayonnaise, peas, carrots etc
sade kahve	Turkish coffee without sugar
sade pilav	plain rice 'pilav'
sahanda yumurta	fried eggs
sahlep	drink made from 'sahlep' root in hot milk and cinnamon
salam	salami
salata	salad
salatalık	cucumber
salça	tomato sauce or paste
salçalı	with tomato sauce
salçalı köfte	meatballs in tomato sauce
salyongoz	snails
sandviç ekmeği	rolls
saray lokması	fried batter dipped in syrup
sardalya	sardines
sarığı burma	'Twisted Turban' - turban-shaped 'baklava'
sarmısak	garlic
sazan	carp
sebze	vegetables
sebze çorbası	vegetable soup
sek şarap	dry wine
semizotu	purslane - a herb mixed in salads or stewed

sıcak	hot, warm
sığır eti	beef
sigara böreği	cigarette-shaped fried pastry filled with cheese, parsley etc
simit	ring-shaped bread covered with sesame seeds
sirke	vinegar
soda	soda water
soğan	onions
soğan dolması	stuffed onions
soğuk	cold
som balığı	salmon
sos	sauce
sosis	sausage
soslu	with sauce
su	water
su böreği	layered pastry
sucuk	Turkish sausage with spices and garlic
sumak	sumac - a herb eaten with kebabs
su muhallebisi	rice flour pudding with rosewater
supanglez	mousse - plain or chocolate
sülün	pheasant
süt	milk
sütlaç	rice pudding
sütlü	with milk
sütlü kahve	coffee with milk
süzme yoğurt	strained yoghurt
şalgam	turnip
şam fıstığı	pistachio nuts
şam tatlısı	dessert with syrup
şarap	wine
şeftali	peaches
şeftali reçeli	peach jam
şeftali suyu	peach juice
şehriye	vermicelli
şehriye çorbası	vermicelli soup with lemon
şehriyeli	with vermicelli
şehriyeli pilav	'pilav' with vermicelli
şeker	sugar, candy
şekerli	with sugar

şekerpare	small cakes with syrup
şerbet	sweetened and iced fruit juices
şıra	grape juice
şiş	cooked on a skewer
şişe	bottle
şiş kebabı	small pieces of lamb grilled on skewers
şiş köfte	grilled meatballs on skewers
şurup	syrup
talaş kebabı	lamb baked in pastry
tarama	roe pâté
tarator	nut and garlic sauce
taratorlu karnabahar	cauliflower with nut and garlic sauce
tarhana çorbası	traditional soup with dried yoghurt, tomato and pimento
tas kebabı	diced lamb with rice
tatar böreği	ravioli
tatlı	sweet, dessert
tatlı şarap	sweet wine
tava(da)	fried
tavşan	rabbit
tavuk	chicken
tavuk çorbası	chicken soup
tavuk göğsü	chicken breast pudding – a dessert
tavuk ızgara	barbecued chicken
tavuklu pilav	chicken and rice
taze	fresh
taze beyaz peynir	fresh white cheese
taze fasulye	runner beans in tomato sauce and olive oil
taze soğan	spring onions
tekir	striped mullet
tel kadayıfı	shredded wheat stuffed with nuts in syrup
terbiye	egg and lemon sauce
terbiyeli	with egg and lemon sauce
terbiyeli haşlama	boiled lamb with egg and lemon sauce
terbiyeli köfte	meatballs with egg and lemon sauce
tereyağı	butter

torik	large tunny
tost	toasted sandwich
tulumba tatlısı	semolina doughnut in syrup
tulum peyniri	goat's milk cheese made in a skin
turna	pike
turp	radish
turşu	pickled vegetables
turşu suyu	juice of pickled vegetables
turunç	Seville oranges
tuz	salt
tuzlu	salty
tükenmez	eggs fried with tomatoes and sweet peppers
türlü	meat and vegetable stew
un helvası	flour 'helva'
uskumru	mackerel
uskumru dolması	stuffed mackerel
üzüm	grapes
vanilya	vanilla
viski	whisky
vişne	black cherries
vişne suyu	black cherry juice
votka	vodka
yağ	oil, fat
yahni	meat stew with onions
yaprak dolması	stuffed vine leaves
yayla çorbası	yoghurt soup
yaz türlüsü	stewed summer vegetables
yengeç	crab
yerfıstığı	peanuts
yeşil mercimek çorbası	green lentil soup
yeşil salata	green salad
yeşil zeytin	green olives
yoğurt	yoghurt
yoğurtlu	with yoghurt
yoğurtlu kebap	kebab with pitta bread and yoghurt
yoğurtlu paça	lamb's trotters with yoghurt and garlic
yumurta	egg
yumurtalı	with egg
zerde	saffron rice dessert

zeytin	olives
zeytinyağı	olive oil
zeytinyağlı	in olive oil (eaten cold)
zeytinyağlı biber dolması	stuffed sweet peppers in olive oil
zeytinyağlı enginar	artichokes in olive oil
zeytinyağlı kereviz	celery in olive oil
zeytinyağlı patlıcan pilavı	rice with aubergines in olive oil
zeytinyağlı pırasa	leeks in olive oil
zeytinyağlı pilaki	red haricot beans in olive oil
zeytinyağlı taze bakla	fresh broad beans in olive oil
zeytinyağlı yaprak dolması	vine leaves stuffed with rice, pine nuts and raisins
zeytinyağlı yeşil fasulye	runner beans cooked in tomatoes and olive oil

SHOPPING

Although the official opening hours for shops are from 9.00 a.m. to 7.00 p.m., Monday to Saturday, it is quite possible, particularly in small towns, to find shops open seven days a week, from early morning till late at night. The numerous grocery stores, 'bakkal' (*bak-kal*), tend to have long opening hours everywhere and sell a variety of goods apart from basic food stuffs.

While bargaining is acceptable in some shops, it is not usual if the goods already have a price tag or if a sign such as 'Pazarlık edilmez' (*pazarluhk edeel-mez*) is displayed. This means 'no bargaining'. However, when it comes to the markets, for which Turkey is justly famous, it is always advisable to bargain and to shop around, asking for prices. Tourists are often invited to drink tea, coffee or soft drinks by the shopkeeper – but this does not put them under any obligation to buy. Bargaining is not a fast process and it is important not to try to hurry proceedings, nor is it advisable to show too much eagerness to buy. Indeed, walking out of the shop may result in a better offer from the shopkeeper.

Foreign books and newspapers are sold at specialist bookshops called 'kitapçı' or 'kitabevi' (*keetap-chuh, ketab-evee*); Turkish newspapers are usually found in grocery stores and on news stands.

USEFUL WORDS AND PHRASES

baker	fırın	*fuhrun*
bargaining	pazarlık	*pazarluhk*
bazaar	pazar, çarşı	*pazar, charshuh*
bookshop	kitapçı	*keetap-chuh*
boutique	butik	*booteek*
butcher	kasap	*kassap*

to buy	satın almak	*satuhn almak*
cake shop	pastane	*pastaneh*
carpet	halı	*haluh*
chemist	eczane	*ej-za-neh*
department store	büyük mağaza	*bew-yewk ma-aza*
fashion	moda	*moda*
fishmonger	balıkçı	*baluhk-chuh*
florist	çiçekçi	*cheechek-chee*
grocer	bakkal	*bak-kal*
ironmonger	nalbur	*nalboor*
ladies' wear	kadın giyim eşyası	*kaduhn ghee-yeem esh-yasuh*
market	pazar, çarşı	*pazar, charshuh*
menswear	erkek giyim eşyası	*erkek ghee-yeem esh-yasuh*
newsagent	gazete bayii	*gazeh-teh ba-yee*
off-licence	içki dükkanı	*eech-kee dewk-kan-nuh*
pharmacy	eczane	*ej-za-neh*
receipt	makbuz	*makbooz*
record shop	plakçı	*plak-chuh*
sale	satış	*satuhsh*
shoe shop	ayakkabıcı	*'eye'-yak-kabuh-juh*
shop	dükkan	*dewk-kan*
to go shopping	alışverişe çıkmak	*aluhsh-vereesheh chuhk-mak*
souvenir shop	turistik eşya dükkanı	*tooreesteek esh-ya dewk-kan-nuh*
special offer	özel indirim	*urzel eendeereem*
to spend	harcamak	*harjamak*
stationer	kırtasiyeci	*kuhr-tassee-yeh-jee*
supermarket	süpermarket	*sewpermarket*
tailor	terzi	*terzee*
till	kasa	*kassa*
toyshop	oyuncakçı	*oyoon-jak-chuh*
travel agent	seyahat acentesi	*sayahat ajentessee*

Can you help me?
Bakar mısınız?
bakar muh-suh-nuhz?

I'd like ...
... istiyorum
... *eesteeyoroom*

Do you have ...?
... var mı?
... *var muh?*

How much is this?
Bu kaç lira?
boo kach leera?

Where is the ... department?
... bölümü nerede?
... *burlewmew neh-reh-deh?*

Do you have any more of these?
Bunlardan başka var mı?
boonlardan bashka var muh?

Have you anything cheaper?
Daha ucuz bir şey var mı?
daha ooj-ooz beer shay var muh?

Have you anything larger?
Daha büyüğü var mı?
daha bew-yew-ew var muh?

Have you anything smaller?
Daha küçüğü var mı?
daha kew-chew-ew var muh?

Does it come in other colours?
Başka renkleri var mı?
bashka renkleree var muh?

Can I try it/them on?
Üstümde deneyebilir miyim?
ewss-tewm-deh deneh-yeh-beeleer mee-yeem?

Where do I pay?
Kasa nerede?
kassa neh-reh-deh?

Can I have a refund?
Paramı geri alabilir miyim?
paramuh gheree alabeeleer mee-yeem?

I'm just looking
Şöyle bir bakıyorum
shurleh beer bakuh-yoroom

I'll come back later
Sonra tekrar geleceğim
sonra tekrar ghel-ejeh-eem

That's far too much
Çok pahalı
chok pahaluh

I'll give you ...
Size ... vereyim
seezeh ... vereh-yeem

That's my last offer
Daha fazla veremem
daha fazla vereh-mem

REPLIES YOU MAY BE GIVEN

Yardım edebilir miyim?
Can I help you?

Daha aşağı olmaz
That's my final offer

Üstünüzde denemek ister misiniz?
Would you like to try it on?

Maalesef mevcudu tükendi
I'm sorry, we're out of stock

Para iade etmiyoruz
We cannot give cash refunds

Bir alacak pusulası verebilirim
I can give you a credit note

Mevcut mallarımız bu kadar
That is all we have

Bozuk para rica edeceğim
Have you got anything smaller?

Özür dilerim, onu bozamayacağım
Sorry, I've no change for that note

OK, I'll take it
Tamam, alıyorum
tamam, aluh-yoroom

SHOPPING

Could you wrap it for me?
Lütfen paket yapar mısınız?
lewtfen paket yapar muh-suh-nuhz?

Can I have a receipt?
Bir makbuz rica ediyorum
beer makbooz reeja edeeyoroom

Can I have a bag please?
Bir torba rica ediyorum
beer torba reeja edeeyoroom

THINGS YOU'LL SEE OR HEAR

antika	antiques
ayakkabı	shoes
aylık taksitler	monthly instalments
bakkaliye	groceries
bölüm	department
buyurun	please, do come in/go ahead etc
büro malzemeleri	office supplies
büyük mağaza	department store
çay	tea
depozito	deposit
dergi	magazine
düzine	dozen
fiat, fiyat	price
gazete	newspaper
güle güle giy!	*means* 'wear it happily'
güle güle kullan!	*means* 'use it happily'
halılar	carpets
içki	spirits

⟶

indirimli satış	sale (reduced prices)
kadın giyim eşyası	ladies' clothes
kafetarya	snackbar
kahve	coffee
kalite	quality
kaliteli	high quality
kapalı çarşı	covered bazaar
kasap	butcher
kasap dükkanı	butcher's shop
kilim	rug
kilogram	kilogram
kira	rental
kitabevi, kitapçı	bookshop
kürk	fur
mallar	goods
moda	fashion
oyuncaklar	toys
özel fiyat	special price
özel indirim	special offer
pastane	cake shop
pazarlık edilmez	no bargaining
satılan mal makbuzu	goods are not exchanged
olmadan değiştirilmez	without receipt
satın alma	purchase
satış	sale
selfservis	self-service
seyahat acentesi	travel agent
sigaracı	tobacconist
şekerleme	confectionery
taksitler	instalments
tatlı yiyecekler	confectionery
tükendi	sold out
ucuz	inexpensive
üst kat	upper floor

AT THE HAIRDRESSER

Turkish hairdressers are similar to those found in most European countries. A range of beauty treatments may also be offered at some ladies' hairdressers.

USEFUL WORDS AND PHRASES

appointment	randevu	*randeh-voo*
beard	sakal	*sakal*
to bleach	rengini açmak	*ren-gheenee ach-mak*
blond	sarışın	*saruh-shuhn*
brush	fırça	*fuhr-cha*
comb	tarak	*tarak*
conditioner	balsam	*balsam*
curlers	bigudi	*beegoodee*
curling tongs	saç maşası	*sach masha-suh*
curly	kıvırcık	*kuh-vuhr-juhk*
dark	koyu renk	*koyoo renk*
fringe	kakül	*ka-kewl*
gel	jel	*jel*
hair	saç	*sach*
haircut	saç tıraşı	*sach tuhrashuh*
(for ladies)	saç kesme	*sach kess-meh*
hairdresser	berber	*berber*
(for ladies)	kuaför	*kwaffur*
hairdryer	saç kurutma makinesi	*sach koorootma makeenessee*
(for ladies)	şesuar	*shessoo-ar*
highlights	meç	*mech*
long	uzun	*oozoon*
moustache	bıyık	*buh-yuhk*
parting	ayırma	*'eye'-yuhr-ma*
perm	perma	*perma*
shampoo	şampuan	*shampooan*

shave	sakal tıraşı	*sakal tuhrash-uh*
shaving foam	tıraş köpüğü	*tuhrash kur-pew-ew*
short	kısa	*kuh-sa*
styling mousse	saç kremi	*sach kremee*
tint	hafif boya	*hafeef boya*
wavy	dalgalı	*dalgaluh*

I'd like to make an appointment
Randevu almak istiyorum
randeh-voo almak eesteeyoroom

Just a trim please
Lütfen biraz uçlarından alın
lewtfen beeraz ooch-laruhndan aluhn

Not too much off please
Lütfen fazla kısaltmayın
lewtfen fazla kuh-saltm-'eye'-yuhn

A bit more off here please
Lütfen burasını biraz daha kısaltın
lewtfen boora-suhnuh beeraz daha kuh-saltuhn

I'd like a cut and blow-dry
Lütfen kesip fönle kurutun
lewtfen kesseep furnleh koorootoon

I'd like a perm
Perma yaptırmak istiyorum
perma yaptuhr-mak eesteeyoroom

I'd like highlights
Meç istiyorum
mech eesteeyoroom

THINGS YOU'LL SEE OR HEAR

arkadan	at the back
ayırma	parting
bahşiş	tip
berber	men's hairdresser
bukle	curl
daha kısa	shorter
enseden	back of the neck
fönle kurutma	blow dry
jilet	razor blade
kesmek	to cut
kısa	short
kuaför	ladies' hairdresser
kuru	dry
mizanpli	set
perçem	fringe
perma	perm
önden	at the front
sakal	beard
tıraş köpüğü	shaving foam
tıraş sabunu	shaving soap
ton vermek	tint
uzun	long
yan	side
yıkamak	to wash
yıkama ve mizanpli	wash and set

SPORTS

The long coastline and very favourable weather conditions provide excellent opportunities for water sports in the summer. Swimming, water-skiing, sailing, and sailboarding are all available. Skin-diving is a popular sport, not least because the Western Aegean coast is full of sunken cities and other marvels. However, a word of caution is necessary with regard to historical relics: it is illegal to take them out of Turkey.

In the winter, skiing is possible in several locations, the most popular of which is Mount Olympus (Uludağ) near Istanbul. There are also many unspoilt mountains and forests for walking and mountaineering. Foreigners may join hunting parties organized by specialist travel agencies, which will provide all the necessary information concerning permits, seasons, weapons and ammunition.

Finally, for those who would rather watch a unique spectacle, there is the traditional Turkish sport of oil wrestling. The wrestlers are covered in olive oil which makes it difficult for the opponents to get a hold on each other. Every July, wrestling championships are held in Kırkpınar outside Edirne.

USEFUL WORDS AND PHRASES

athletics	atletizm	*atleteezm*
badminton	badminton	*badmeenton*
ball	top	*top*
beach	plaj	*plaj*
bicycle	bisiklet	*beesseeklet*
canoe	kano	*kano*
deckchair	şezlong	*shezlong*
to dive	dalmak	*dalmak*
diving board	tramplen	*tramplen*
fishing	balık avlama	*baluhk avlama*

fishing rod	olta kamışı	*olta kamuhshuh*
football	futbol	*footbol*
football match	futbol maçı	*footbol machuh*
golf	golf	*golf*
golf course	golf sahası	*golf sahassuh*
gymnastics	jimnastik	*jeemnasteek*
hunting	avcılık	*av-juhluhk*
jogging	koşu	*koshoo*
lake	göl	*gurl*
racket	raket	*raket*
riding	binicilik	*beeneejeeleek*
rowing boat	kayık	*k- 'eye'-yuhk*
to run	koşmak	*koshmak*
sailboard	yelkenli sörf	*yelkenlee surf*
sailing	yelkencilik	*yelkenjeeleek*
sand	kum	*koom*
sea	deniz	*deneez*
skiing	kayak	*k- 'eye'-yak*
sledge	kızak	*kuhzak*
snorkel	şnorkel	*shnorkel*
snow	kar	*kar*
stadium	stadyum	*stad-yoom*
to swim	yüzmek	*yewzmek*
swimming pool	yüzme havuzu	*yewzeh havoozoo*
tennis	tenis	*teneess*
tennis court	tenis kortu	*teneess kortoo*
tennis racket	tenis raketi	*teneess raketee*
tent	çadır	*chaduhr*
Turkish	yağlı güreş	*ya-luh ghewresh*
wrestling		
volleyball	voleybol	*voleh-bol*
walking	yürüyüş	*yewrew-yewsh*
waterskiing	su kayağı	*soo k-'eye'-ya-uh*
water skis	su kayağı	*soo k-'eye'-ya-uh*
wave	dalga	*dalga*
winter sports	kış sporları	*kuhsh sporlaruh*
yacht	yat	*yat*

How do I get to the beach?
Plaja nereden gidilir?
plaja neh-reh-den gheedeeleer?

How deep is the water here?
Burada suyun derinliği ne kadar?
boorada soo-yoon dereenlee-ee neh kadar?

Is there an indoor/outdoor pool here?
Burada kapalı/açık havuz var mı?
boorada kapaluh/achuhk havooz var muh?

Is it safe to swim here?
Burada emniyetle yüzülebilir mi?
boorada emnee-yetleh yewzewleh-beeleer mee?

Can I fish here?
Burada balık tutabilir miyim?
boorada baluhk tootabeeleer mee-yeem?

Do I need a licence?
İzin belgesi lazım mı?
eezeen belghessee la-zuhm muh?

I would like to hire a bike
Bir bisiklet kiralamak istiyorum
beer beesseeklet keeralamak eesteeyoroom

How much does it cost per hour/day?
Bir saatlik/günlük kirası ne kadar?
beer sa-atleek/ghewnlewk keerassuh neh kadar?

Where can I hire ...?
Nerede ... kiralayabilirim?
neh-reh-deh ... keeral-'eye'-yabeeleereem?

THINGS YOU'LL SEE OR HEAR

açık yüzme havuzu	open-air swimming pool
avcılık	hunting
balık tutmak yasaktır	no fishing
bisikletçi	cyclist
dağcılık	mountaineering
dalmak	to dive
dalma techizatı	skin-diving equipment
girmek yasaktır	no entry, keep out
ilk yardım	first aid
kapalı yüzme havuzu	indoor swimming pool
kar	snow
kiralık bisiklet	bicycle hire
kiralık kayık	boat hire
kürek çekmek	to row
liman	port
marina	marina
orman	forest
ski yapmak	skiing
spor tesisleri	sporting facilities
su sporları	water sports
su kayağı	water-skiing
tehlike	danger
tehlikeli akıntı	dangerous current
yağlı güreş	oil wrestling
yasak	forbidden
yelkencilik	sailing
yelkenli	sailing boat
yürümek	to walk
yürüyüş	walking
yüzmek	to swim
yüzmek yasaktır	no swimming

POST OFFICES AND BANKS

Post offices are generally open from 8.30a.m. until 5.30p.m. Monday to Friday, but close for one hour at noon. Main post offices stay open until late into the night and maintain a skeleton service on Saturdays and Sundays. They are easily recognizable by their yellow PTT signs. Post-restante facilities are available at main (Merkez) post offices. Letter boxes in Turkey are painted yellow.

Banks are open from 8.30 to 12.00 and from 1.30 to 5.00 Monday to Friday. The basic unit of Turkish currency is the Lira. The symbol for it, TL, is placed after the amount, e.g. 5000. -TL.

USEFUL WORDS AND PHRASES

airmail	uçak postası	*oochak postassuh*
bank	banka	*banka*
banknote	banknot	*banknot*
to change	değiştirmek, bozmak	*deh-eeshteermek, bozmak*
cheque	çek	*chek*
collection	boşaltma	*boshaltma*
counter	gişe	*gheesheh*
customs form	gümrük formüleri	*ghewm-rewk formewleree*
delivery	teslim	*tessleem*
exchange rate	döviz kuru	*durveez kooroo*
form	formüler	*formewler*
letter	mektup	*mektoop*
letter box	mektup kutusu	*mektoop kootoosoo*
mail	posta	*posta*
main post office	merkez postanesi	*merkez postanessee*
money order	havale	*havaleh*
package	paket	*paket*
parcel	koli	*kolee*
post	posta	*posta*
postage rates	posta ücretleri	*posta ewj-retleree*

83

postal order	posta havalesi	*posta havalessee*
postcard	posta kartı,	*posta kartuh,*
	kartpostal	*kartpostal*
postcode	posta kodu	*posta kodoo*
poste-restante	postrestant	*post-restant*
postman	postacı	*postajuh*
post office	postane	*postaneh*
pound sterling	İngiliz Sterlini	*eengheeleez sterleenee*
registered letter	taahhütlü mektup	*ta-ah-hewtlew*
stamp	pul	*pool*
telegram	telgraf	*telgraf*
telephone	telefon	*telefon*
telephone box	telefon kabini	*telefon kabeenee*
token	jeton	*jeton*
traveller's	seyahat çeki	*sayahat chekee*
cheque		

How much is a letter to ...?
...-e mektup ücreti ne kadar?
...-eh mektoop ewj-retee neh kadar?

I would like to send a postcard to ...
...-e bir posta kartı göndermek istiyorum
...-eh beer posta kartuh gurn-dermek eesteeyoroom

I would like three 70 lira stamps
Üç adet 70 Liralık pul rica ediyorum
ewch adet yetmeesh leeraluhk pool reeja edeeyoroom

I want to register this letter
Bu mektubu taahhütlü göndermek istiyorum
boo mektooboo ta-ah-hewtlew gurn-dermek eesteeyoroom

I want to send this parcel to ...
Bu koliyi ...-e göndermek istiyorum
boo kolee-yee ...-eh gurn-dermek eesteeyoroom

How long does the post to … take?
…-e ne kadar zamanda varır?
…-eh neh kadar zamanda varuhr?

Where can I post this?
Bunu nereden postalayabilirim?
boonoo neh-reh-den postal-'eye'-ya-beeleereem?

I want to make an international call
Bir milletlerarası telefon konuşması yapmak istiyorum
beer meel-letler-arassuh telefon konoosh-massuh yapmak eesteeyoroom

Is there any mail for me?
Bana mektup var mı?
bana mektoop var muh?

I'd like to send a telegram
Bir telgraf göndermek istiyorum
beer telgraf gurn-dermek eesteeyoroom

This is to go airmail
Bu uçak postası ile gidecek
boo oochak postassuh eeleh gheedejek

I'd like to change this into lira
Bunu Türk Lirasına çevirmek istiyorum
boonoo tewrk leerassuhna cheveermek eesteeyoroom

Can I cash these traveller's cheques here?
Bu seyahat çeklerini burada bozdurabilir miyim?
boo sayahat cheklereenee boorada bozdoora-beeleer mee-yeem?

What is the rate for the pound?
İngiliz Sterlininin kuru nedir?
eengheeleez sterleeneeneen kooroo nedeer?

THINGS YOU'LL SEE OR HEAR

açık	open
adres	address
az miktarlarda pul	stamps in small quantities
banka	bank
cadde	street
doldurunuz	fill in
gişe	counter
gönderen	sender
gönderilen	addressee
havale	money order
ikamet adresi	domicile
kambiyo	exchange, bureau de change
kapalı	closed
kartpostal	postcard
kasa	cashdesk
koli	parcel
koli gişesi	parcels counter
küçük paket	small packet
matbua	printed matter
mektup	letter
memur	official
merkez postanesi	central post office
mesai saatleri	opening hours
müteakip boşaltma	next collection
numara	number *(house)*
otomatik arama	direct dialling
paket	packet, package
posta kartı	postcard
postane	post office
PTT	posta, telefon, telgraf
pul	stamp
sokak	street

⟶

taahhütlü mektup	registered mail
telefon	telephone
telefon kabini	telephone box
telgraf	telegram
uçakla	airmail
uçak postası	airmail
yıldırım telgraf	express telegram
yurtdışı posta ücretleri	overseas postage rates
yurtiçi posta ücretleri	inland postal rate

REPLIES YOU MAY BE GIVEN

Pasaportunuzu görebilir miyim, lütfen?
Can I see your passport please?

Maalesef ... kabul etmiyoruz
I'm afraid we don't accept ...

TELEPHONING

The telephone system in Turkey is operated by the post office (PTT) and is still unsatisfactory by European standards. Public telephone boxes are few and far between and are generally concentrated in the central areas of large cities. This deficiency is corrected to some extent by public call boxes installed by small shops and restaurants which display a sign (Telefon). To use a public telephone you will need special tokens called 'jeton'. These 'jeton' come in three sizes: large, medium and small – for international, intercity and local calls respectively – and can be bought in post offices.

Direct dialling is possible only from larger cities and towns, as well as from some tourist resorts. Otherwise calls have to be put through the operator. To dial direct to the UK from Turkey you must first dial 9 to obtain the distinct STD tone. After this dial 944 (omitting the 0 which prefixes all UK numbers). To call the USA dial 9-91. Calls through the operator may be made 'normal' (*normal*), urgent 'acele' (*ajeleh*) or very urgent 'yıldırım' (*yuhl-duh-ruhm*).

The tones you hear differ slightly from those heard on British phones; a repeated long tone means that the number is ringing, while alternating shorter tones indicate an engaged number.

USEFUL WORDS AND PHRASES

call	telefon konuşması	*telefon konoosh-massuh*
to call	telefon etmek	*telefon etmek*
code	kod numarası	*kod noomarassuh*
to dial	çevirmek	*cheveer-mek*
dialling tone	çevir sesi	*cheveer sessee*
emergency	imdat	*eemdat*
engaged	meşgul	*mesh-gool*
enquiries	danışma servisi	*danushma serveessee*

extension	dahili	*daheelee*
international call	milletlerarası konuşma	*meel-letler-arassuh konoosh-massuh*
large token	büyük jeton	*bew-yewk jeton*
medium token	orta jeton	*orta jeton*
number	numara	*noomara*
operator	santral memuru	*santral memooroo*
pay-phone	umumi telefon	*oomoomee telefon*
push-button phone	düğmeli telefon	*dew-melee telefon*
receiver	ahize	*aheezeh*
reverse charge call	ödemeli konuşma	*urdemelee konooshma*
ringing tone	telefon çalıyor tonu	*telefon chaluh-yor tonoo*
small token	küçük jeton	*kew-chewk jeton*
telephone	telefon	*telefon*
telephone box	telefon kulübesi	*telefon koolew-bessee*
telephone directory	telefon rehberi	*telefon rehberee*
token	jeton	*jeton*
wrong number	yanlış numara	*yanluhsh noomara*

Where is the nearest phone box?
En yakın telefon kulübesi nerede?
en yakuhn telefon koolew-bessee neh-reh-deh?

Is there a telephone directory?
Telefon rehberi var mı?
telefon rehberee var muh?

Can I have a token/three tokens for ...?
... için bir/üç jeton verir misiniz?
... eecheen beer/ewch jeton vereer meesseeneez?

I would like the directory for ...
... telefon rehberini rica ediyorum
... *telefon rehbereenee reeja edeeyoroom*

Can I call abroad from here?
Buradan yurtdışına telefon edebilir miyim?
booradan yoort-duhshuhna telefon edebeeleer mee-yeem?

How much is a call to ...?
...-ya telefon ücreti ne kadardır?
...-ya telefon ewj-retee neh kadar-duhr?

I would like to reverse the charges
Ödemeli konuşmak istiyorum
urdemelee konooshmak eesteeyoroom

I would like a number in ...
...-deki bir numarayı arıyorum
...-dekee beer noomara-yuh aruh-yoroom

I'd like to make a normal call to ...
... numara ile normal konuşma yapmak istiyorum
... *noomara eeleh normal konooshma yapmak eesteeyoroom*

Hello, this is ... speaking
Alo, ben ...
alo, ben ...

Is that ...?
... ile mi görüşüyorum?
... eeleh mee gurewshew-yoroom?

Speaking
Benim
bencem

I would like to speak to ...
... ile görüşmek istiyorum
... eeleh gurewsh-mek eesteeyoroom

Extension ... please
Dahili numarayı istiyorum
daheelee noomara-yuh eesteeyoroom

Please tell him ... called
Lütfen, kendisine ... aradı deyin
lewtfen, kendeesseeneh ... araduh day-yeen

Ask him to call me back please
Lütfen beni aramasını söyleyin
lewtfen benee aramassuhnuh surlay-yeen

My number is ...
Benim numaram ...
beneem noomaram ...

Do you know where he is?
Nerede olduğunu biliyor musunuz?
neh-reh-deh oldoo-oonoo beeleeyor moo-soonooz?

When will he be back?
Ne zaman dönecek?
neh zaman durnejek?

Could you leave him a message?
Bir mesaj bırakabilir miyim?
beer messaj buhrakabeeleer mee-yeem?

I'll ring back later
Sonra tekrar ararım
sonra tekrar araruhm

91

Sorry, wrong number
Affedersiniz, yanlış numara
af-federseeneez, yanluhsh noomara

REPLIES YOU MAY BE GIVEN

Benim
Speaking

Kendisi şimdi burada yoklar
Sorry, he's not in

Kiminle görüşüyorum?
Who's calling?

Numaranız kaç?
What's your number?

Sizi arasın mı?
Can he call you back?

Kiminle görüşmek istiyorsunuz?
Who do you want to speak to?

Yanlış numara çevirdiniz
You've got the wrong number

Saat ...-de dönecek
He'll be back at ...

92

THINGS YOU'LL SEE OR HEAR

acele	urgent
ahize	receiver, handset
arıza servisi	faults service
atınız	insert
bekleyiniz	wait
bozuk	out of order
bozuk para	coins
çeviriniz	dial
çevir tonu	dial tone
dahili	extension
itfaiye	fire brigade
jeton	telephone token(s)
kadran	dial
kaldırınız	lift (the receiver)
kısa konuşunuz!	be brief!
mandal	hook
meslekler rehberi	yellow pages
meşgul	engaged
milletlerarası	international
santral memuru	operator
şehirlerarası konuşma	long-distance call
tarife	charges
telefon	telephone
telefon kodu	dialling code
telefon konuşması	call, conversation
telefon numarası	telephone number
telefon rehberi	telephone directory
yangın	fire
yerel konuşma	local call
yıldırım	very urgent
yurtdışı	abroad

HEALTH

You are advised to take out full medical insurance to cover the costs of possible treatment in Turkey. In Istanbul there are a number of foreign hospitals, and many doctors in Turkish hospitals speak a foreign language.

Chemists operate on a rota system which ensures that there is always one chemist open in a town or district at all times. All chemists display a board showing where this duty chemist is located. Turkish chemists are qualified to treat minor injuries.

USEFUL WORDS AND PHRASES

accident	kaza	*kaza*
AIDS	AIDS	*aydz*
ambulance	ambülans, cankurtaran	*ambewlanss, jankoortaran*
anaemia	kansızlık, anemi	*kanssuhz-luhk, anemee*
antibiotic	antibiyotik	*antee-beeyoteek*
appendicitis	apandisit	*apandeesseet*
appendix	kör bağırsak	*kur ba-uhrssak*
aspirin	aspirin	*aspeereen*
asthma	astım	*astuhm*
backache	sırt ağrısı	*surt a-ruhssuh*
bandage	sargı	*sarguh*
bite	sokma	*sokma*
bladder	mesane	*messaneh*
to bleed	kanamak	*kanamak*
blister	kabarcık	*kabarjuhk*
blood	kan	*kan*
blood donor	kan verici	*kan vereejee*
burn	yanık	*yanuhk*
cancer	kanser	*kanser*

chemist	eczacı	*ejzajuh*
chickenpox	suçiçeği	*soocheecheh-ee*
cold	soğuk algınlığı	*so-ook alguhnluh-uh*
concussion	beyin sarsıntısı	*beh-yeen*
		sarssuhn-tuhssuh
constipation	kabızlık	*kabuhzluhk*
corn	nasır	*nasuhr*
cough	öksürük	*urksew-rewk*
cut	kesik	*kesseek*
dentist	dişçi	*deesh-chee*
diabetes	şeker hastalığı	*sheker hastaluh-uh*
diarrhoea	ishal	*eeshal*
dizzy	baş dönmesi	*bash durn-messee*
doctor	doktor	*doktor*
earache	kulak ağrısı	*koolak a-ruhssuh*
fever	ateş	*atesh*
filling	dolgu	*dolgoo*
first aid	ilk yardım	*eelk yarduhm*
flu	grip	*greep*
fracture	kırık	*kuhruhk*
German measles	kızamıkçık	*kuhzamuhk-chuhk*
glasses	gözlük	*gurzlewk*
haemorrhage	kanama	*kanama*
hayfever	saman nezlesi	*saman nezlessee*
headache	baş ağrısı	*bash a-ruhssuh*
heart attack	kalp krizi	*kalp kreezee*
hepatitis	hepatit	*hepateet*
hip	kalça	*kalcha*
hospital	hastane	*hastaneh*
ill	hasta	*hasta*
indigestion	hazımsızlık	*hazuhm-suhzluhk*
inflammation	iltihap	*eelteehap*
injection	enjeksiyon, iğne	*enjeksseeyon, ee-neh*
injury	yaralanma	*yaralanma*
to itch	kaşınmak	*kashuhn-mak*

jaw	çene	*cheneh*
kidney	böbrek	*burbrek*
lung	akciğer	*akjee-er*
lump	yumru	*yoomroo*
measles	kızamık	*kuhzamuhk*
migraine	migren	*meegren*
mumps	kabakulak	*kabakoolak*
nausea	mide bulantısı	*meedeh boolantuhssuh*
neck	boyun	*boyoon*
nurse	hasta bakıcı	*hasta bakuhjuh*
ointment	merhem	*merhem*
operation	ameliyat	*amelee-yat*
optician	göz doktoru	*gurz doktoroo*
pain	ağrı	*a-ruh*
painkiller	ağrı giderici	*a-ruh gheedereejee*
penicillin	penisilin	*penesseeleen*
pharmacy	eczane	*ejzaneh*
pill	hap	*hap*
plaster *(sticky)*	plaster	*plaster*
plaster of Paris	alçı	*alchuh*
pneumonia	zatürree	*zatewr-reh*
pregnant	hamile	*hameeleh*
prescription	reçete	*recheteh*
rash	isilik	*eesseeleek*
rheumatism	romatizma	*romateezma*
scald	yanık	*yanuhk*
scratch	bere	*bereh*
sling	askı	*asskuh*
smallpox	çiçek hastalığı	*cheechek hastaluh-uh*
sore	ağrı	*a-ruh*
sore throat	boğaz ağrısı	*bo-az a-ruhssuh*
splinter	çatlama	*chatlama*
sprain	burkulma	*boorkoolma*
sting	yanma	*yanma*
stomach	mide	*meedeh*

temperature *(fever)*	ateş	*atesh*
tonsils	bademcik	*bademjik*
tooth	diş	*deesh*
toothache	diş ağrısı	*deesh a-ruhssuh*
travel sickness	yol tutması	*yol tootmassuh*
ulcer	ülser	*ewlsser*
vaccination	aşı	*ashuh*
to vomit	kusmak	*koossmak*
whooping cough	boğmaca	*bo-maja*
wound	yara	*yara*

I have a pain in ...
...-de bir ağrı var
...-deh beer a-ruh var

I do not feel well
Kendimi iyi hissetmiyorum
kendeemee ee-yee heess-setmeeyoroom

I feel faint
Halsizlik duyuyorum
halseezleek doo-yoo-yoroom

I feel sick
Midem bulanıyor
meedem boolanuhyor

I feel dizzy
Başım dönüyor
bashuhm durnew-yor

It hurts here
Burası acıyor
boorassuh ajuhyor

HEALTH

It's a sharp pain
Bıçak gibi bir ağrı
buhchak gheebee beer a-ruh

It's a dull pain
Devamlı bir sızı
devamluh beer suhzuh

It hurts all the time
Sürekli ağrıyor
sewreklee a-ruhyor

It only hurts now and then
Arada sırada ağrıyor
arada suhrada a-ruhyor

It hurts when you touch it
Dokunduğunuz zaman acıyor
dokoondoo-oonooz zaman ajuhyor

It hurts more at night
Geceleri daha fazla ağrıyor
ghejeleree daha fazla a-ruhyor

It stings
Yanıyor
yanuhyor

It aches
Sızlıyor
suhzluhyor

I have a temperature
Ateşim var
atesheem var

I need a prescription for ...
... için bir reçete istiyorum
... *eecheen beer recheteh eesteeyoroom*

I normally take ...
Normal olarak ... alıyorum
normal olarak ... aluhyoroom

I'm allergic to ...
...-e allerjim var
...-eh allerjeem var

Have you got anything for ...?
... için bir şey var mı?
... eecheen beer shay var muh?

Do I need a prescription for ...?
... için reçete lazım mı?
... eecheen recheteh la-zuhm muh?

I've lost a filling
Dolgu düştü
dolgoo dewsh-tew

REPLIES YOU MAY BE GIVEN

Günde üç defa ikişer tablet alınız
Take two tablets three times a day

Suyla/çiğnemek için
With water/for chewing

Günde bir/iki/üç defa
Once/twice/three times a day

Yalnız yatacağınız zaman
Only when you go to bed

Sabahları kahvaltıdan önce
First thing in the morning

Normal olarak hangi ilaçları alıyorsunuz?
What medicines do you usually take?

Bence bir doktora görünmeniz gerekiyor
I think you should see a doctor

Maalesef ondan bizde yok
I'm sorry, we don't have that

O ilaç için doktordan reçete almanız lazım
For that you need a prescription

Onu burada bulamazsınız
You can't get that here

Geçmiş olsun!
Get well soon!

THINGS YOU'LL SEE OR HEAR

acil vaka	emergency
bekleme salonu	waiting room
cankurtaran	ambulance
çocuk doktoru	paediatrician
dispanser	out-patients' clinic
dişçi	dentist
göz doktoru	optician
hastalık sigortası	health insurance
hastane	hospital
hekim	doctor
ilk yardım	first aid
jinekolog	gynaecologist
kulak, burun ve boğaz	ear, nose and throat
muayene	examination
muayenehane	surgery
mütehassıs	specialist
nöbetçi eczane/doktor	duty chemist/doctor
ortopedi uzmanı	orthopaedist
özel bakım ünitesi	intensive care unit
özel hasta	private patient
poliklinik	out-patients' clinic
randevu	appointment
reçete	prescription
reçete ile satılır	prescription only
reçete yazmak	to prescribe
tedavi	treatment

CONVERSION TABLES

DISTANCES

Distances are marked in kilometres. To convert kilometres to miles, divide the km. by 8 and multiply by 5 (one km. being five-eighths of a mile). Convert miles to km. by dividing the miles by 5 and multiplying by 8. A mile is 1609m. (1.609km.).

km.	miles or km.	miles
1.61	**1**	0.62
3.22	**2**	1.24
4.83	**3**	1.86
6.44	**4**	2.48
8.05	**5**	3.11
9.66	**6**	3.73
11.27	**7**	4.35
12.88	**8**	4.97
14.49	**9**	5.59
16.10	**10**	6.21

Other units of length:

1 centimetre	= 0.39 in.	1 inch	= 25.4 millimetres
1 metre	= 39.37 in.	1 foot	= 0.30 metre (30 cm.)
10 metres	= 32.81 ft.	1 yard	= 0.91 metre

WEIGHTS

The unit you will come into most contact with is the kilogram (kilo), equivalent to 2 lb. 3 oz. To convert kg. to lbs., multiply by 2 and add one-tenth of the result (thus, 6 kg. x 2 = 12 + 1.2, or 13.2 lbs). One ounce is about 28 grams, and 1 lb. is 454 g.

grams	ounces		ounces	grams
50	1.76		1	28.3
100	3.53		2	56.7
250	8.81		4	113.4
500	17.63		8	226.8

| | | lbs. | |
kg.		or kg.	lbs.
0.45		1	2.20
0.91		2	4.41
1.36		3	6.61
1.81		4	8.82
2.27		5	11.02
2.72		6	13.23
3.17		7	15.43
3.63		8	17.64
4.08		9	19.84
4.53		10	22.04

TEMPERATURE

To convert centigrade or Celsius degrees into Fahrenheit, the accurate method is to multiply the °C figure by 1.8 and add 32. Similarly, to convert °F to °C, subtract 32 from the °F figure and divide by 1.8. This will give you a truly accurate conversion, but takes a little time in mental arithmetic! See the table below.

°C	°F		°C	°F	
-10	14		25	77	
0	32		30	86	
5	41		36.9	98.4	body temperature
10	50		40	104	
20	68		100	212	boiling point

LIQUIDS

Motorists from the UK will be used to seeing petrol priced per litre (and may even know that one litre is about 1¾ pints). One 'imperial' gallon is roughly 4½ litres, but USA drivers must remember that the American gallon is only 3.8 litres (1 litre = 1.06 US quart). In the following table, imperial gallons are used:

litres	gals. or l.	gals.
4.54	1	0.22
9.10	2	0.44
13.64	3	0.66
18.18	4	0.88
22.73	5	1.10
27.27	6	1.32
31.82	7	1.54
36.37	8	1.76
40.91	9	1.98
45.46	10	2.20
90.92	20	4.40
136.38	30	6.60
181.84	40	8.80
227.30	50	11.00

TYRE PRESSURES

lb./sq.in.	15	18	20	22	24
kg./sq.cm.	1.1	1.3	1.4	1.5	1.7

lb./sq.in.	26	28	30	33	35
kg./sq.cm.	1.8	2.0	2.1	2.3	2.5

MINI-DICTIONARY

about: about 16 yaklaşık onaltı
accelerator gaz pedalı
accident kaza
accommodation kalacak yer
ache ağrı
adaptor *(electrical)* adaptör
address adres
adhesive tutkal
Aegean Ege
after sonra
after-shave tıraş losyonu
again gene
against karşı
air-conditioning klima
aircraft uçak
air freshener oda spreyi
air hostess hostes
airline havayolu
airport havalimanı
Albania Arnavutluk
Albanian *(person, adj)* Arnavut
alcohol alkol
all bütün
   all the streets bütün sokaklar
   that's all, thanks hepsi bu
   kadar, teşekkür ederim
almost hemen hemen
alone yalnız
already şimdiden
always hep
ambulance cankurtaran
America Amerika
American *(person)* Amerikalı
   (adj) Amerikan
ancient site tarihi yer
and ve
ankle ayak bileği
anorak anorak
another *(different)* başka

(further) daha
anti-freeze antifriz
antique antika
antique shop antikacı
antiseptic antiseptik
apartment daire
aperitif aperitif
appetite iştah
apple elma
application form başvuru formu
appointment randevu
apricot kayısı
aqualung balıkadam hava
   tüpü
arm kol
art sanat
art gallery sanat galerisi
artist sanatçı
as: as soon as possible en kısa
   zamanda
ashtray kül tablası
Asia Asya
asleep: he's asleep uyuyor
aspirin aspirin
at: at the post office postanede
   at night geceleyin
   at 3 o'clock saat üçte
Athens Atina
attractive cazip
aunt teyze
Australia Avustralya
Australian *(person)* Avustralyalı
Austria Avusturya
automatic otomatik
away: is it far away? uzak mı?
   go away! git!
awful berbat
axe balta
axle aks

105

baby bebek
baby-sitter çocuk bakıcısı
back *(not front)* arka
  (of body) sırt
backgammon tavla
bad kötü
bait yem
bake pişirmek
baker fırıncı
balcony balkon
ball top
  (dance) balo
ball-point pen tükenmez
  kalem
banana muz
band *(musicians)* orkestra
bandage sargı
bank banka
banknote banknot
bar bar
  bar of chocolate tablet
  çikolata
barbecue ızgara
barber's berber
basement bodrum
basin *(sink)* lavabo
basket sepet
bath banyo
  to have a bath yıkanmak
bathing hat bone
bathroom banyo
battery pil
beach plaj
beans fasulye
beard sakal
beautiful güzel
because çünkü
bed yatak
bed linen yatak çarşafları
bedroom yatak odası
beef sığır eti
beer bira

before önce
beginner acemi
behind arkada
beige bej
Belgium Belçika
bell *(church)* çan
  (door) zil
belly-dancing göbek dansı,
  oryantal dans
below altında
belt kemer
beside yanında
best en iyi
better daha iyi
between arasında
bicycle bisiklet
big büyük
bikini bikini
bill hesap
bin liner çöp torbası
bird kuş
birthday doğum günü
  happy birthday! doğum
  gününüz kutlu olsun!
birthday present doğum günü
  hediyesi
biscuit bisküvi
bite *(verb)* ısırmak
  (by insect) sokma
bitter acı
black siyah
blackberry böğürtlen
Black Sea Karadeniz
blanket battaniye
bleach *(verb: hair)* rengini
  açmak
  (noun) ağartıcı madde
blind *(cannot see)* kör
  (on window) istor
blister kabarcık
blood kan
blouse bluz

blue mavi
boat gemi
  (smaller) kayık
body vücut
boil kaynatmak
  (on body) çıban
bolt *(verb)* sürgülemek
  (noun: on door) sürgü
bone kemik
bonnet *(car)* kaporta
book *(noun)* kitap
  (verb) yer ayırtmak
booking office bilet gişesi
bookshop kitapçı
boot *(car)* bagaj
  (footwear) çizme
border sınır
boring sıkıcı
born: I was born in ...
  ...-de doğdum
Bosphorus İstanbul Boğazı
both her ikisi
both of them her ikisi de
  both of us her ikimiz de
  both ... and ... hem ...
  hem de ...
bottle şişe
bottle-opener şişe açacağı
bottom alt
  (of sea) dip
bowl kase
box kutu
boy oğlan
boyfriend erkek arkadaş
bra sütyen
bracelet bilezik
braces pantalon askısı
brake *(noun)* fren
  (verb) fren yapmak
brandy konyak
bread ekmek
breakdown *(car)* arıza

(nervous) sinir krizi
breakfast kahvaltı
breathe nefes almak
  I can't breathe nefes
  alamıyorum
bridge köprü
briefcase evrak çantası
British İngiliz
brochure broşür
broken kırık
  (out of order) bozuk
  broken leg kırık bacak
brooch broş
brother erkek kardeş
brown kahverengi
bruise çürük
brush *(noun)* fırça
  (verb) fırçalamak
bucket kova
building bina
Bulgaria Bulgaristan
Bulgarian *(person)* Bulgar
bumper tampon
burglar hırsız
burn *(verb)* yanmak
  (noun) yanık
bus otobüs
bus station otobüs terminali
business iş
  it's none of your business
  seni ilgilendirmez
busy *(person, telephone)*
  meşgul
  (crowded) kalabalık
but ama
butcher kasap
butter tereyağı
button düğme
buy satın almak
by: by the window pencerenin
  yanında
  by Friday Cumaya kadar

by myself tek başıma
Byzantine Bizans

cabbage lahana
cable car teleferik
cagoule naylon yağmurluk
cake pasta
calculator hesap makinesi
call: what's this called?
   bunun adı nedir?
camel deve
camera fotoğraf makinesi
campsite kamping
camshaft kam mili
can *(tin)* teneke kutu
   can you come? gelebilir
   misiniz?
Canada Kanada
Canadian *(person)* Kanadalı
cancer kanser
candle mum
canoe kano
cap *(bottle)* kapak
   (hat) kasket
car otomobil
caravan karavan
carburettor karbüratör
card kart
cardigan hırka
careful dikkatli
   be careful! dikkat et!
carpet halı
carriage *(train)* vagon
carrot havuç
carry-cot portbebe
case valiz
cash nakit para
   (coins) bokuz para
   to pay cash nakit ödemek
cassette kaset
cassette player kasetli teyp

castle kale
cat kedi
cauliflower karnabahar
cave mağara
cemetery mezarlık
centre merkez
certificate belge
chair iskemle
chambermaid oda hizmetçisi
chamber music oda müziği
change *(noun: money)* bozuk
   para
   (verb: clothes) üstünü
   değiştirmek
cheap ucuz
cheers! şerefe!
cheese peynir
chemist *(shop)* eczane
cheque çek
cheque book çek defteri
cherry kiraz
chess satranç
chest göğüs
chewing gum çiklet
chicken tavuk
child çocuk
children çocuklar
china porselen
China Çin
Chinese *(person)* Çinli
chips patates kızartması
chocolate çikolata
   box of chocolates bir kutu
   çikolata
chop *(food)* pirzola
   (to cut) doğramak
Christian Hıristiyan
Christian name öz ad
church kilise
cigar puro
cigarette sigara
cinema sinema

city şehir
city centre şehir merkezi
class sınıf
classical music klasik müzik
clean temiz
clear *(obvious)* açık
  (water) duru
  is that clear? anlaşıldı mı?
clever akıllı
clock saat
  (alarm) çalar saat
close *(near)* yakın
  (stuffy) havasız
  (verb) kapatmak
  the shop is closed dükkan
  kapalı
clothes giyim eşyası
club kulüp
  (cards) sinek
clutch debriyaj
coach yolcu otobüsü
  (of train) yolcu vagonu
coach station otogar
coat palto
coathanger askı
cockroach hamamböceği
coffee kahve
coin madeni para
cold *(illness)* soğuk algınlığı
  (adj) soğuk
collar yaka
collection *(stamps etc)*
  koleksiyon
colour renk
colour film renkli filim
comb *(noun)* tarak
  (verb) taramak
come gelmek
  I come from ... ...-den
  geliyorum
  we came last week geçen
  hafta geldik

come here! buraya gel!
communication cord imdat
freni
compartment kompartıman
complicated karmaşık
concert konser
conditioner *(hair)* balsam
conductor *(bus)* biletçi
  (orchestra) şef
congratulations! tebrikler!
constipation kabızlık
consulate konsolosluk
contact lenses kontak lensleri
contraceptive gebeliği önleyici
cook *(noun)* ahçı
  (verb) pişirmek
cooking utensils kap kaçak
cool serin
copper bakır
cork mantar
corkscrew tirbuşon
corner köşe
corridor koridor
cosmetics makyaj malzemesi
cost *(noun)* fiyat
  what does it cost? fiyatı ne
kadar?
cotton wool idrofil pamuk
cough *(verb)* öksürmek
  (noun) öksürük
country *(state)* ülke
  (not town) kır
cousin *(male)* kuzen
  (female) kuzin
crab pavurya
cramp kramp
crayfish kerevit
cream *(for cake etc)* krema
  (lotion) krem
credit card kredi kartı
Crete Girit
crew mürettebat

crisps cips
crowded kalabalık
cruise deniz gezisi
crutches koltuk değnekleri
cry *(weep)* ağlamak
  (shout) bağırmak
cucumber salatalık
cufflinks kol düğmesi
cup fincan
cupboard dolap
curlers bigudi
curls bukle
curtain perde
Customs Gümrük
cut *(noun)* kesik
  (verb) kesmek
Cyprus Kıbrıs

dad baba
dairy *(shop)* sütçü dükkanı
damp nemli
dance dans
dangerous tehlikeli
dark karanlık
  (colour) koyu
Dardanelles Çanakkale
  Boğazı
daughter kız
day gün
dead ölü
deaf sağır
dear *(person)* değerli
  (expensive) pahalı
deckchair şezlong
deep derin
deliberately kasten
dentist dişçi
dentures protez
deny inkar etmek
  I deny it reddediyorum
deodorant deodoran

department store büyük
  mağaza
departure kalkış
develop *(a film)* develope etmek
diamond *(jewel)* elmas
  (cards) karo
diarrhoea ishal
diary günce
dictionary sözlük
die ölmek
diesel dizel
different başka
  that's different o başka
  I'd like a different one bir
  başkasını istiyorum
difficult zor
dining room yemek salonu
dinner akşam yemeği
dirty kirli
disabled sakat
distributor *(in car)* distribütör
dive dalmak
diving board tramplen
divorced boşanmış
do yapmak
doctor doktor
document belge
dog köpek
doll bebek
dollar dolar
door kapı
down aşağı
drawing pin raptiye
dress elbise
drink *(verb)* içmek
  (soft drink) içecek
  (alcoholic) içki
  would you like a drink? bir
  şey içmek ister misiniz?
drinking water içme suyu
drive *(verb)* sürmek
driver şoför

driving licence şoför ehliyeti
drunk sarhoş
dry kuru
dry cleaner kuru
  temizleyici
dummy *(for baby)* emzik
during sırasında
dustbin çöp tenekesi
duster toz bezi
duty-free gümrüksüz

each tanesi
  twenty liras each tanesi yirmi
  lira
early erken
earring küpe
ears kulaklar
east doğu
easy kolay
egg yumurta
either: either of them ikisinden
  biri
  either ... or ... ya ... ya ...
elastic elastiki
elastic band lastik bant
elbow dirsek
electric elektrikli
electricity elektrik
else: something else başka bir
  şey
someone else başka birisi
  somewhere else başka bir
  yerde
embarrassing utandırıcı
embassy elçilik
embroidery nakış
emerald zümrüt
emergency acil durum
empty boş
end son
engaged *(couple)* nişanlı

(occupied) meşgul
engine *(motor)* motor
England İngiltere
English İngiliz
  (language) İngilizce
Englishman İngiliz
Englishwoman İngiliz kadını
enlargement büyültme
enough yeter
entertainment eğlence
entrance giriş
envelope zarf
escalator yürüyen merdiven
especially özellikle
Europe Avrupa
evening akşam
every her
everyone herkes
everything her şey
everywhere her yerde
example örnek
  for example örneğin
excellent mükemmel
excess baggage fazla bagaj
exchange *(verb)* değiştirmek
exchange rate döviz kuru
excursion gezinti
excuse me! affedersiniz!
exit çıkış
expensive pahalı
explain açıklamak
extension lead uzatma kablosu
eye göz
eye drops göz damlası
eyes gözler

face yüz
faint *(unclear)* belirsiz
  (verb) bayılmak
  to feel faint halsizlik
  duymak

fair *(funfair)* panayır
  (just) haklı
  it's not fair bu haksızdır
false teeth takma dişler
family aile
fan *(ventilator)* vantilatör
  (enthusiast) hayran
fan belt vantilatör kayışı
far uzak
  how far is ...? ... ne kadar
  uzaktadır?
fare taşıma ücreti
farm çiftlik
farmer çiftçi
fashion moda
fast hızlı
fat *(adj)* şişman
  (on meat etc) yağ
father baba
feel *(touch)* dokunmak
  I feel hot çok sıcak
  I feel like ... ... istiyorum
  I don't feel well kendimi iyi
  hissetmiyorum
feet ayaklar
felt-tip pen keçe uçlu kalem
ferry feribot, araba vapuru
fever ateş
fez fes
fiancé(e) nişanlı
field tarla
fig incir
filling *(tooth)* dolgu
  (sandwich etc) iç
film filim
filter filtre
finger parmak
fire ateş
  (blaze) yangın
fire extinguisher yangın
  söndürme aleti
firework hava fişeği

first birinci
first aid ilk yardım
first floor birinci kat
fish balık
fishing balık tutmak
  to go fishing balık avına
  çıkmak
fishing rod olta kamışı
fishmonger balıkçı
fizzy gazlı
flag bayrak
flash *(camera)* flaş
flat *(level)* düz
  (apartment) daire
flavour tat
flea pire
flight uçuş
flip-flops tokyo
flippers paletler
flour un
flower çiçek
flu grip
flute flüt
  (reed) ney
fly *(verb)* uçmak
  (insect) sinek
fog sis
folk dance halk oyunu
folk music halk müziği
food yiyecek
food poisoning gıda
  zehirlenmesi
foot ayak
football futbol
  (ball) top
for için
  for me benim için
  what for? niçin?
  for a week bir hafta için
foreigner yabancı
forest orman
fork çatal

fortnight iki hafta
fountain çeşme
fourth dördüncü
fracture kırık
France Fransa
free serbest
   (no cost) bedava
freezer buzluk
French *(language)* Fransızca
Frenchman Fransız
Frenchwoman Fransız kadını
fridge buzdolabı
friend arkadaş
friendly dost
from: from ... to ...
   ...-den ...-e
front: in front of ... ...-in
   önünde
frost don
fruit meyva
fruit juice meyva suyu
fry kızartmak
frying pan tava
full dolu
   I'm full doydum
full board tam pansiyon
funnel *(for pouring)* huni
funny komik
   (odd) acayip
furniture mobilya

garage garaj
   (petrol station) benzin
   istasyonu
garden bahçe
garlic sarmısak
gas-permeable lenses hava
   geçiren lensler
gay *(happy)* şen
   (homosexual) homoseksüel
gear vites

gear lever vites kolu
gents *(toilet)* erkekler tuvaleti
German *(person)* Alman
Germany Almanya
get *(fetch)* getirmek
   have you got ...? ... var mı?
   to get the train trene binmek
get back: we get back
   tomorrow yarın dönüyoruz
   to get something back
   bir şeyi geri almak
get in girmek
   (arrive) varmak
get out çıkmak
get up *(rise)* kalkmak
gift hediye
gin cin
girl kız
girlfriend kız arkadaş
give vermek
glad memnun
   I'm glad memnunum
glass cam
   (to drink) bardak
glasses gözlük
gloss prints parlak tab
gloves eldiven
glue zamk
go gitmek
   I'm going to Istanbul
   İstanbul'a gidiyorum
goggles koruyucu gözlük
gold altın
good iyi
goodbye hoşça kal
government hükümet
granddaughter kız torun
grandfather büyükbaba
grandmother büyükanne
grandson torun
grapes üzüm
grass ot

Great Britain Büyük Britanya
Greece Yunanistan
Greek *(person)* Yunanlı
  (ethnic Greek) Rum
  (language) Rumca
Greek orthodox Rum Ortodoks
  Kilisesi
green yeşil
grey gri
grill ızgara
grocer *(shop)* bakkal
ground floor zemin kat
ground sheet su geçirmez
  yaygı
guarantee *(noun)* garanti
  (verb) garanti etmek
guard muhafız
  (train) kondüktör
guide book rehber
guitar gitar
gun *(rifle)* tüfek
  (pistol) tabanca

hair saç
haircut *(for man)* saç tıraşı
  (for woman) saç kesme
hairdresser kuaför
hair dryer saç kurutma
  makinası
hair spray saç spreyi
half yarım
  half an hour yarım saat
half board yarım pansiyon
ham jambon
hamburger hamburger
hammer çekiç
hand el
handbag el çantası
hand brake el freni
handkerchief mendil
handle *(door)* kapı tokmağı

handsome yakışıklı
hangover içki sersemliği
happy mutlu
harbour liman
hard sert
  (difficult) zor
hard lenses sert lensler
hat şapka
have: I don't have ... ...-im
  yok
  I don't have a ticket biletim
  yok
  can I have ...? ... istiyorum
  do you have ...? ... var mı?
  I have to go now şimdi
  gitmem lazım
hayfever saman nezlesi
he o
head baş
headache baş ağrısı
headlights farlar
headscarf başörtüsü
hear duymak
hearing aid işitme cihazı
heart kalp
heart attack kalp krizi
heating ısıtma
heavy ağır
heel topuk
hello merhaba
help *(noun)* yardım
  (verb) yardım etmek
  help! imdat!
her o
  it's her odur
  it's for her onun için
  give it to her ona ver
  her house/her shoes
  onun evi/onun ayakkabıları
  this is hers bu onun
high yüksek
highway code trafik kanunu

hill tepe
him o
  it's him odur
  it's for him onun için
  give it to him ona ver
hire kiralamak
his: his book/his shoes
  onun kitabı/onun ayakkabıları
  this is his bu onun
history tarih
hitch-hike otostop yapmak
hobby merak
holiday tatil, bayram
Holland Hollanda
honest dürüst
honey bal
honeymoon balayı
hookah nargile
horn *(car)* klakson
  (animal) boynuz
horrible korkunç
hospitable konuksever
hospital hastane
hot sıcak
  (spicy) acı
hour saat
house ev
how? nasıl?
hungry: I'm hungry acıktım
hurry: I'm in a hurry acelem
  var
husband koca

I ben
ice buz
ice cream dondurma
ice cube parça buz
if eğer
ignition ateşleme
ill hasta
immediately hemen

impossible imkansız
in -da, -de
  in Istanbul Istanbul'da
  in my room odamda
  in English İngilizcede
India Hindistan
Indian *(person)* Hintli
  (adj) Hint
indicator gösterge
indigestion hazımsızlık
infection enfeksiyon
information bilgi
  (travel) danışma
injection enjeksiyon
injury yaralanma
ink mürekkep
inner tube iç lastik
insect böcek
insect repellent böcek
  ilacı
insomnia uykusuzluk
insurance sigorta
interesting ilginç
interpret tercüme etmek
invitation davet
Iran İran
Iraq Irak
Ireland İrlanda
Irishman İrlandalı
Irishwoman İrlandalı kadın
iron *(metal)* demir
  (for clothes) ütü
ironmonger nalbur
Islam İslam
Islamic İslami
island ada
it o
Italy İtalya
itch *(noun)* kaşıntı
  it itches kaşınıyor

jacket ceket
jam reçel
jazz caz
jealous kıskanç
 he is jealous kıskanıyor
jeans blucin
jellyfish denizanası
jeweller kuyumcu
job iş
jog *(verb)* koşmak
 to go for a jog koşuya
 çıkmak
joke şaka
journey seyahat
jumper kazak
just: it's just arrived şimdi
 geldi
 I've just one left yalnız bir
 tane kaldı

kebab kebap
key anahtar
kidney böbrek
kilo kilo
kilometre kilometre
kiss *(noun)* öpücük
kitchen mutfak
knee diz
knife bıçak
knit örmek
know: I don't know
 bilmiyorum
Koran Kur'an

label etiket
lace dantel
laces *(of shoe)* ayakkabı bağları
ladies *(toilet)* bayanlar tuvaleti
lady hanım, bayan
lake göl

lamb kuzu
lamp lamba
lampshade abajur
land *(not sea)* kara
 (verb) (aeroplane) inmek
 (from boat) karaya çıkmak
language dil
large büyük
last *(final)* son
 last week geçen hafta
 last month geçen ay
 at last! en sonunda!
late: it's getting late
 geç oldu
 the bus is late otobüs geç
 kaldı
laugh gülmek
launderette otomatlı
 çamaşırhane
laundry *(place)* çamaşırhane
 (dirty clothes) kirli çamaşır
laxative müshil
lazy tembel
leaf yaprak
leaflet broşür
learn öğrenmek
leather deri
leave *(go away)* ayrılmak
 (object) bırakmak
left *(not right)* sol
 there's nothing left hiç bir
 şey kalmadı
left luggage emanet
leg bacak
lemon limon
lemonade limonata
 (fizzy) gazoz
length uzunluk
lens mercek
less daha az
lesson ders
letter mektup

letterbox mektup kutusu
lettuce marul
library kütüphane
licence izin belgesi
life hayat
lift *(in building)* asansör
  could you give me a lift?
  beni de alabilir misiniz?
light *(not heavy)* hafif
  (not dark) aydınlık
light meter pozometre
lighter çakmak
lighter fuel çakmak benzini
like: I like you senden
  hoşlanıyorum
  I like swimming yüzmeyi
  seviyorum
  it's like ... ... gibi
lime *(fruit)* misket limonu
lip salve dudak merhemi
lipstick ruj
liqueur likör
lira lira
list liste
litre litre
litter çöp
little *(small)* küçük
  it's a little big biraz
  büyük
  just a little azıcık
liver karaciğer
lobster istakoz
long uzun
  how long does it take? ne
  kadar sürer?
lorry kamyon
lost property kayıp eşya
lot: a lot çok
loud yüksek sesle
  (colour) çiğ
lounge salon
love *(noun)* sevgi

(verb) sevmek
lover sevgili
low alçak
luck şans
luggage bagaj
luggage rack bagaj rafı
lunch öğle yemeği

magazine dergi
mail posta
make yapmak
make-up makyaj
man adam
manager yönetici
map harita
  a map of Istanbul İstanbul
  şehir planı
marble mermer
margarine margarin
market çarşı
marmalade portakal reçeli
married evli
mascara rimel
mast direk
match *(light)* kibrit
  (sport) maç
material *(cloth)* kumaş
mattress şilte
maybe belki
me: it's me benim
  it's for me benim için
  give it to me bana ver
meal yemek
meat et
mechanic makinist
medicine ilaç
  (science) tıp
Mediterranean *(noun)* Akdeniz
meeting toplantı
melon kavun
menu yemek listesi

message mesaj
midday öğleyin
middle: in the middle ortada
midnight gece yarısı
milk süt
minaret minare
mine: this is mine bu benim
mineral water maden suyu
minute dakika
mirror ayna
mistake hata
  to make a mistake hata
  yapmak
monastery manastır
money para
month ay
monument anıt
moon ay
moped moped
more daha
morning sabah
  in the morning sabahleyin
mosaic mozaik
Moslem Müslüman
mosque cami
  Blue Mosque Sultan Ahmet
  Camisi
mosquito sivrisinek
mother anne
motorbike motosiklet
motorboat motorbot
motorway ekspresyol
mountain dağ
mouse fare
moustache bıyık
mouth ağız
move hareket etmek
  don't move! kımıldama!
  (house) taşınmak
movie filim
Mr. Bay
Mrs. Bayan

much: not much fazla değil
  much better çok daha
  iyi
mug kulplu bardak
mule katır
mum anne
museum müze
mushroom mantar
music müzik
musical instrument müzik
  aleti
musician müzisyen
mussels midye
mustard hardal
my: my bag/my keys
  benim çantam/benim
  anahtarlarım
mythology mitoloji

nail *(metal)* çivi
  (finger) tırnak
nail file tırnak törpüsü
nail polish tırnak cilası
name ad
nappy çocuk bezi
narrow dar
near: near the door kapının
  yakınında
  near London Londra
  yakınında
necessary gerekli
necklace kolye
need *(verb)* lazım olmak
  I need ... bana ... lazım
  there's no need gerek yok
needle iğne
negative *(photo)* negatif
neither: neither of them hiç
  biri
  neither ... nor ... ne ...
  ne de ...

nephew yeğen
never asla
new yeni
news haber
newsagent gazete bayii
newspaper gazete
New Zealand Yeni Zelanda
New Zealander Yeni
  Zelandalı
next bir sonraki
  next week gelecek hafta
  next month gelecek ay
nice hoş
niece yeğen
night gece
nightclub gece kulübü
nightdress gecelik
no *(response)* hayır
  I have no money param
  yok
noisy gürültülü
north kuzey
Northern Ireland Kuzey
  İrlanda
nose burun
not değil
notebook not defteri
nothing hiç bir şey
novel roman
now şimdi
nowhere hiç bir yerde
nude çıplak
nudist camp çıplaklar kampı
number sayı
  (telephone) numara
number plate plaka
nurse hasta bakıcı
nut *(fruit)* fıstık
  (for bolt) somun

occasionally arada sırada

octopus ahtapot
of -in
  the name of the village
  köyün adı
office ofis
often sık sık
oil yağ
ointment merhem
OK tamam
old eski
  (of persons) yaşlı
olive zeytin
omelette omlet
on -da, -de
  on the beach plajda
  on the terrace terasta
  a book on Turkey Türkiye
  hakkında bir kitap
one bir
onion soğan
only yalnız
open *(verb)* açmak
  (adj) açık
opposite: opposite the hotel
  otelin karşısında
optician gözlükçü
or veya
orange *(colour)* turuncu
  (fruit) portakal
orange juice portakal suyu
orchestra orkestra
ordinary *(normal)* olağan
our bizim
  this is ours bu bizim
out: he's out dışarı çıktı
outside dışarıda
over üzerinde
  over there orada
overtake geçmek
oyster istiridye

pack of cards iskambil
destesi
package ambalaj
(parcel) paket
packet paket
  a packet of ... bir paket ...
padlock asma kilit
page sayfa
pain ağrı
paint *(noun)* boya
pair çift
Pakistan Pakistan
Pakistani Pakistanlı
pale soluk
pancakes gözleme
paper kağıt
  (newspaper) gazete
paracetamol parasetamol
parcel koli
pardon? efendim?
parents ana baba
park *(noun)* park
  (verb) park etmek
party *(celebration, political)* parti
  (group) grup
passenger yolcu
passport pasaport
pasta makarna
path yol
pavement kaldırım
pay ödemek
peach şeftali
peanuts yerfıstığı
pear armut
pearl inci
peas bezelye
pedestrian yaya
peg *(for clothes)* mandal
pen dolma kalem
pencil kurşun kalem
pencil sharpener kalemtıraş
penfriend mektup arkadaşı

peninsula yarımada
penknife çakı
people halk
pepper *(& salt)* karabiber
  (red/green) biber
peppermints nane şekeri
per: per night geceliği
perfect mükemmel
perfume parfüm
perhaps belki
perm perma
petrol benzin
petrol station benzin istasyonu
petticoat jüpon
photograph *(noun)* fotoğraf
  (verb) fotoğraf çekmek
photographer fotoğrafçı
phrase book yabancı dil kılavuzu
piano piyano
pickpocket yankeseci
picnic piknik
piece parça
pillow yastık
pilot pilot
pin toplu iğne
pine *(tree)* çam
pineapple ananas
pink pembe
pipe *(for smoking)* pipo
  (for water) boru
pizza pizza
place yer
plant bitki
plaster *(for cut)* plaster
plastic plastik
plastic bag naylon torba
plate tabak
platform platform
  (trains) peron
play *(theatre)* oyun
pleasant hoş
please lütfen

plug (*electrical*) fiş
  (*sink*) tıkaç
pocket cep
poison zehir
police polis
policeman polis
police station karakol
politics politika
poor yoksul
  (*bad quality*) kalitesiz
pop music pop müziği
pork domuz eti
port (*harbour*) liman
porter (*for luggage*) hamal
  (*hotel*) kapıcı
possible mümkün
post (*noun*) posta
  (*verb*) postalamak
post box posta kutusu
postcard kartpostal
poster afiş
post office postane
postman postacı
potato patates
poultry kümes hayvanları
pound (*money*) lira
  (*weight*) libre
powder toz
  (*make-up*) pudra
pram çocuk arabası
prawn karides
  (*bigger*) büyük karides
prescription reçete
pretty (*beautiful*) güzel
  (*quite*) oldukça
priest rahip
private özel
problem sorun
  what's the problem? sorun
  nedir?
public halka açık
pull çekmek

puncture lastik patlaması
purple mor
purse para çantası
push itmek
pushchair puset
pyjamas pijama

quality kalite
quay rıhtım
question soru
queue (*noun*) kuyruk
  (*verb*) kuyruğa girmek
quick çabuk
quiet sessiz
quite (*fairly*) oldukça
  (*fully*) tamamen

radiator radyatör
radio radyo
radish turp
railway line demiryolu hattı
rain yağmur
raincoat yağmurluk
raisins kuru üzüm
rare (*uncommon*) nadir
  (*steak*) az pişmiş
rat sıçan
razor blade jilet
read okumak
reading lamp masa lambası
  (*bed*) başucu lambası
ready hazır
rear lights arka sinyal
  lambaları
receipt makbuz
receptionist resepsiyoncu
record (*music*) plak
  (*sporting etc*) rekor
record player pikap
record shop plakçı dükkanı

red kırmızı
refreshments meşrubat
registered letter taahhütlü
  mektup
relative *(noun)* akraba
relax dinlenmek
religion din
remember hatırlamak
  I don't remember
  hatırlamıyorum
rent *(verb)* kiralamak
reservation rezervasyon
rest *(remainder)* kalan
  (relaxation) dinlenme
restaurant restoran
restaurant car vagon restoran
return geri dönmek
Rhodes Rodos
rice *(cooked)* pilav
  (uncooked) pirinç
rich zengin
right *(correct)* doğru
  (direction) sağ
ring *(to call)* telefon etmek
  (wedding etc) yüzük
ripe olgun
river nehir
road yol
rock *(stone)* kaya
  (music) rok müziği
roll *(bread)* sandviç ekmeği
  (verb) yuvarlanmak
roller skates patenler
roof dam
  (flat) taraça
room oda
  (space) yer
rope ip
rose gül
round *(circular)* yuvarlak
  it's my round sıra bende
rowing boat kayık

rubber *(eraser)* silgi
  (material) lastik
rubbish çöp
ruby *(stone)* yakut
rucksack sırt çantası
rug *(mat)* kilim
  (blanket) battaniye
ruins harabeler
ruler *(for drawing)* cetvel
rum rom
Rumania Romanya
Rumanian
  (person, adj) Romen
run *(person)* koşmak
runway pist
Russia Rusya
Russian *(person, adj)* Rus

sad üzgün
safe emniyetli
safety emniyet
sailing boat yelkenli
salad salata
salami salam
sale *(at reduced prices)* indirimli
  satış
salmon som balığı
salt tuz
same: the same ... aynı ...
  same again please lütfen gene
  aynısından
samovar semaver
sand kum
sandals sandal
sand dunes kumullar
sandwich sandviç
sanitary towels femil
sauce sos
saucepan tencere
sauna sauna
sausage sosis
say söylemek

what did you say? ne dedin?
how do you say ...? ... nasıl
denir?
scarf atkı
(head) eşarp, başörtüsü
school okul
scissors makas
Scotland İskoçya
Scottish İskoç
screw vida
screwdriver tornavida
sea deniz
seafood deniz ürünleri
seat oturacak yer
seat belt emniyet kemeri
second (adj) ikinci
see görmek
I can't see göremiyorum
I see anlıyorum
sell satmak
send göndermek
separate ayrı
separated ayrılmış
sellotape® seloteyp
serious ciddi
serviette peçete
several birkaç
sew dikmek
shampoo şampuan
shave (noun) tıraş
(verb) tıraş olmak
shaving foam tıraş köpüğü
shawl şal
she o
sheet çarşaf
shell (on beach) deniz kabuğu
ship gemi
shirt gömlek
shoe ayakkabı
shoe laces ayakkabı bağları
shoe polish ayakkabı cilası
shop dükkán

shopping alışveriş
to go shopping alışverişe
çıkmak
short kısa
shorts şort
shoulder omuz
shower (bath) duş
(rain) sağanak
shrimp karides
shutter (camera) obdüratör
(window) kepenk
sick (ill) hasta
I feel sick midem bulanıyor
side (edge) kenar
I'm on her side ben ondan
yanayım
sidelights borda fenerleri
sights: the sights of ...
...-nın görmeye değer yerleri
silk ipek
silver (colour) gümüş rengi
(metal) gümüş
simple basit
sing şarkı söylemek
single (one) tek
(unmarried) bekar
sister kız kardeş
skid (verb) kaymak
skin cleanser cilt temizleyici
skirt eteklik
sky gök
sleep (noun) uyku
(verb) uyumak
to go to sleep uykuya dalmak
sleeping bag uyku tulumu
sleeping pill uyku ilacı
slippers terlikler
slow yavaş
small küçük
smell (noun) koku
(verb) (give off smell) kokmak
(detect smell) koklamak

smile *(noun)* gülümseme
  (verb) gülümsemek
smoke *(noun)* duman
  (verb) sigara içmek
snack hafif yemek
snorkel şnorkel
snow kar
so: so good o kadar iyi
  not so much o kadar değil
soaking solution *(for contact lenses)* koruyucu sıvı
socks çoraplar
soda water maden sodası
soft lenses yumuşak kontak lensleri
somebody birisi
somehow her nasılsa
something bir şey
sometimes bazen
somewhere bir yerde
son oğul
song şarkı
soon kısa zamanda
sorry! pardon!
  I'm sorry özür dilerim
soup çorba
sour ekşi
south güney
South Africa Güney Afrika
South African *(person)* Güney Afrikalı
souvenir hatıra
spade *(shovel)* bel
  (cards) maça
Spain İspanya
Spanish *(adj)* İspanyol
spanner somun anahtarı
spares yedek
spark(ing) plug buji
speak konuşmak
  do you speak ...? ... biliyor musunuz?

I don't speak ...
  ... bilmiyorum
speed hız
speed limit hız tahdidi
speedometer kilometre saati
spider örümcek
spinach ıspanak
spoon kaşık
sprain burkulma
spring *(mechanical)* yay
  (season) ilkbahar
stadium stadyum
staircase merdiven
stairs merdivenler
stamp pul
stapler tel zımba
star yıldız
start başlangıç
  (verb) başlamak
station istasyon
statue heykel
steak biftek
steal çalmak
  it's been stolen çalındı
steering wheel direksiyon
stewardess hostes
sting *(noun)* sokma
  (verb) sokmak
  it stings yanıyor
stockings çoraplar
stomach mide
stomach-ache karın ağrısı
stop *(verb)* durmak
  (bus stop) durak
  stop! dur!
storm fırtına
strawberry çilek
stream *(small river)* dere
street sokak
string *(cord)* ip
  (guitar etc) tel
student öğrenci

stupid aptal
suburbs banliyö
sugar şeker
suit *(noun)* takım elbise
  (verb) yakışmak
  it suits you sana yakışıyor
suitcase valiz
sun güneş
sunbathe güneşlenmek
sunburn güneş yanığı
sunglasses güneş gözlüğü
sunny: it's sunny hava
  güneşli
suntan bronz ten
suntan lotion güneş losyonu
supermarket süpermarket
supplement ek
surname soyadı
sweat *(noun)* ter
  (verb) terlemek
sweatshirt svetşört
sweet *(not sour)* tatlı
  (candy) şeker
swimming costume mayo
swimming pool yüzme havuzu
swimming trunks mayo
Swiss *(person)* İsviçreli
switch *(noun)* anahtar
Switzerland İsviçre
synagogue sinagog
Syria Suriye
Syrian *(person, adj)* Suriyeli

table masa
tablet tablet
take almak
take-off kalkış
take off *(verb)* kalkmak
talcum powder talk pudrası
talk *(noun)* konuşma
  (verb) konuşmak

tall *(person)* uzun boylu
  (thing) yüksek
tampon tampon
tangerine mandalina
tap musluk
tapestry duvar halısı
taxi taksi
tea çay
team takım
tea towel kurulama bezi
telegram telgraf
telephone *(noun)* telefon
  (verb) telefon etmek
telephone box telefon kulübesi
telephone call telefon konuşması
television televizyon
temperature *(heat)* sıcaklık
  (fever) ateş
temple tapınak
tent çadır
tent peg çadır kazığı
tent pole çadır direği
than: larger than ... ...-den
  büyük
thank *(verb)* teşekkür etmek
  thanks teşekkürler
  thank you teşekkür ederim
that: that bus/that man o
  otobüs/o adam
  that woman o kadın
  what's that? o nedir?
  I think that ... sanıyorum ki ...
their: their room onların odası
  their books onların kitapları
  this is theirs bu onların
them: it's them onlar
  it's for them onlar için
  give it to them onlara ver
then o zaman
there orada
  there is ... ... var
  there is not ... ... yok

thermal spring kaplıca
thermos flask termos
these: these things bu şeyler
 these are mine bunlar
 benimdir
they onlar
thick kalın
thin ince
thing şey
think düşünmek
 I think so bence öyle
 I'll think about it düşüneyim
third üçüncü
thirsty: I'm thirsty susadım
this: this bus/this woman
 bu otobüs/bu kadın
 what's this? bu nedir?
 this is Mr ... bu Bay ...-dir
those: those things o şeyler
 those are his onlar onundur
throat boğaz
throat pastilles boğaz pastilleri
through içinden
 through the town şehrin
 içinden
thumb başparmak
thunderstorm gök gürültülü
 fırtına
ticket bilet
tie *(noun)* kravat
 (verb) bağlamak
tights külot çorap
time zaman
 what's the time? saat kaç?
timetable tarife
tin teneke kutu
tin opener konserve açacağı
tip *(money)* bahşiş
 (end) uç
tired yorgun
 I feel tired yorgunum
tissues kağıt mendil

to: to England İngiltere'ye
 to the station istasyona
 to the doctor doktora
toast tost
tobacco tütün
today bugün
toe ayak parmağı
together birlikte
toilet tuvalet
toilet paper tuvalet kağıdı
tomato domates
tomato juice domates suyu
tomorrow yarın
tongue dil
tonic tonik
tonight bu gece
too *(also)* de
 (excessively) fazla
tooth diş
toothache diş ağrısı
toothbrush diş fırçası
toothpaste diş macunu
torch el feneri
tour tur
tourist turist
towel havlu
tower kule
town şehir
town hall belediye sarayı
toy oyuncak
track suit eşofman
tractor traktör
tradition gelenek
traffic trafik
traffic jam trafik tıkanıklığı
traffic lights trafik lambası
trailer römork
train tren
translate tercüme etmek
transmission *(for car)*
 transmisyon
travel agency seyahat acentesi

traveller's cheque seyahat
çeki
tray tepsi
tree ağaç
trousers pantalon
Troy Truva
try denemek
tunnel tünel
Turk *(person)* Türk
Turkey Türkiye
Turkish Türk
  (language) Türkçe
Turkish bath hamam
Turkish coffee Türk kahvesi
Turkish delight lokum
turquoise *(stone)* firuze
tweezers cımbız
typewriter daktilo
tyre lastik

umbrella şemsiye
uncle amca
under altında
underpants külot
university üniversite
unmarried bekar
until kadar
unusual olağandışı
up yukarı
  (upwards) yukarıya
urgent acil
us: it's us biziz
  it's for us bizim için
  give it to us bize ver
use *(noun)* kullanım
  (verb) kullanmak
  it's no use faydasız
useful faydalı
usual olağan
usually genellikle

vacancy *(room)* boş oda
vacuum flask termos
valley vadi
valve valf
vanilla vanilya
vase vazo
veal dana eti
vegetables sebze
vegetarian *(person)* etyemez
vehicle taşıt
very çok
  very much çok
vest fanila
view manzara
viewfinder vizör
villa villa
village köy
vinegar sirke
violin keman
visa vize
visit *(noun)* ziyaret
  (verb) ziyaret etmek
visitor konuk
vitamin tablet vitamin hapı
vodka votka
voice ses

wait beklemek
waiter garson
  waiter! garson!
waiting room bekleme salonu
waitress garson
Wales Galler Ülkesi
walk *(noun)* yürüyüş
  (verb) yürümek
  to go for a walk yürüyüşe
çıkmak
walkman® walkman
wall duvar
wallet cüzdan
war savaş

wardrobe gardırop
warm sıcak
washing powder deterjan
washing-up liquid bulaşık
  deterjanı
wasp yabanarısı
watch *(noun)* saat
  (verb) seyretmek
water su
waterfall çağlayan
waterpipe *(to smoke)* nargile
wave *(noun)* dalga
  (verb) sallamak
we biz
weather hava
wedding düğün
week hafta
wellingtons lastik çizme
Welsh Gal'li
west batı
wet ıslak
what? ne?
wheel tekerlek
wheelchair tekerlekli sandalye
when? ne zaman?
where? nerede?
which? hangi?
whisky viski
white beyaz
who? kim?
why? neden?
wide geniş
wife hanım
wind rüzgar
window pencere
windscreen ön cam
wine şarap
wine list şarap listesi
wing kanat
with ile
  with sugar şekerli
without -siz

without sugar şekersiz
woman kadın
wood *(forest)* orman
  (material) tahta
wool yün
word kelime
work *(noun)* iş
  (verb) çalışmak
worry beads tespih
worse daha kötü
worst en kötü
wrapping paper ambalaj kağıdı
wrist bilek
write yazmak
writing paper yazı kağıdı
wrong yanlış

year yıl
yellow sarı
yes evet
yesterday dün
yet henüz
  not yet henüz değil
yoghurt yoğurt
you *(sing. polite and plural)* siz
  (sing. familiar) sen
your: your book *(polite)* sizin
  kitabınız
  (familiar) senin kitabın
yours: is it yours?
  (polite) sizin mi?
  (familiar) senin mi?
youth hostel gençlik yurdu
Yugoslavia Yugoslavya
Yugoslav(ian) Yugoslav

zip fermuar
zoo hayvanat bahçesi